A.B.S

Days of Heaven on Earth

A BOOK OF DAILY DEVOTIONAL
READINGS FROM SCRIPTURE TEXTS
AND LIVING TRUTH

CHRISTIAN PUBLICATIONS
Camp Hill, Pennsylvania

Days of Heaven on Earth

✝ *The mark of vibrant faith*

CHRISTIAN PUBLICATIONS
Publishing House of The Christian and Missionary Alliance
3825 Hartzdale Drive, Camp Hill PA 17011

Library of Congress Catalog Card No. 84-70150
© 1984 by Christian Publications. All rights reserved
ISBN: 0-87509-246-9
Printed in the United States of America

THE DAYS OF HEAVEN

The days of heaven are peaceful days,
   Still as yon glassy sea;
So calm, so still in God, our days,
   As the days of heaven would be.

The days of heaven are holy days,
   From sin forever free;
So cleansed and kept our days, O Lord,
   As the days of heaven would be.

The days of heaven are happy days.
   Sorrow they never see;
So full of gladness all our days,
   As the days of heaven would be.

The days of heaven are healthful days,
   They feed on life's fair tree;
So feeding on Thy strength, O Christ,
   Our days as heaven may be.

Walk with us, Lord, thro' all the days,
   And let us walk with Thee;
Till as Thy will is done in heaven,
   On earth so shall it be.

Preface

Most of Albert B. Simpson's many books are sermons—sermons preached to large, enthusiastic audiences, stenographically recorded, lightly edited and pressed into print.

Days of Heaven on Earth (or *Days of Heaven upon Earth,* as the title read in the original 1897 edition) is somewhat different. In response to repeated requests for a daily devotional, Simpson himself prepared this book, selecting appropriate passages from various of his books, pamphlets and sermons.

Days of Heaven met with instant approval. The book went through many printings and continues today to be one of Simpson's most popular titles. This new edition has been carefully edited and contemporized in the hope that the essential message God gave this great leader a century ago will capture the hearts of a new generation hungry for the deeper life in Christ Jesus.

H. Robert Cowles
Executive Vice-President
Christian Publications

Redeeming the time—Ephesians 5:16.

Two little words are found in the Greek version here—*ton kairon.* They are translated in the revised version, "Buying up for yourselves the opportunity." The two words *ton kairon* mean, literally, the opportunity.

They do not refer to time in general, but to a special point in time, a juncture, a crisis. They refer to a moment full of possibilities quickly passing by, which we must seize and make the best of before it has passed away.

It is intimated that there are not many such moments of opportunity, because the days are evil. These moments are like flowers which appear here and there in the barren desert: pluck them while you can. Or they are like a business opportunity which comes once in a lifetime; buy it up while you have the chance. Be spiritually alert; *be not unwise, but understanding what the will of the Lord is* (v. 16). *Walk circumspectly, not as fools, but as wise* (v. 15), buying up for yourselves the opportunity.

Sometimes it is a moment of time to be saved; sometimes a soul to be led to Christ; sometimes it is an occasion for love; sometimes for patience; sometimes for victory over temptation and sin. Let us redeem it.

....

I will . . . cause you to walk in my stat-utes—Ezekiel 36:27.

The highest spiritual condition is one where life is spontaneous and flows without effort, like the deep floods of Ezekiel's river, where the struggles of the swimmer ceased, and he was borne by the current's resistless force.

So God leads us into spiritual conditions and habits which become the spontaneous impulses of our being, and we live and move in the fullness of the divine life.

These spiritual habits are not the outcome of some transitory impulse, but often are acquired and established slowly. They begin, like every true habit, in a definite act of will, and they are confirmed by the repetition of that act until it becomes a habit. The first stages always involve effort and choice. We have to take a stand and hold it steadily, and after we have done so a certain time, it becomes second nature and carries us by its own force.

The Holy Spirit is willing to form such habits in every direction of our Christian lives. If we will obey Him in the first steps of faith, we will soon become established in the attitude of obedience, and duty will be delight.

Watch and pray—Matthew 26:41.

We need to watch our prayers as well as watch for the answers to our prayers. It requires as much *wisdom* to pray rightly as it does *faith* to receive the answers to our prayers.

A Christian confided that he had been in years of darkness because God had failed to answer certain of his prayers. As a result, he had been in a state bordering on infidelity.

A very few moments were sufficient to convince this friend that his prayers had been entirely unauthorized and that God had never promised to answer such prayers. They were for things which, in the exercise of ordinary wisdom, he should have accomplished himself. The result was deliverance from the cloud of unbelief which was almost wrecking his Christian life.

There are some things about which we do not need to pray as much as to take the light which God has already given. Many people are asking God to give them peculiar signs, tokens and supernatural intimations of His will. Our business is to use the light He has given, and then He will give whatever more we need.

Blessed is the man—Psalm 1:1.

Three things are notable about this blessed man:

1. His company. He *walketh not in the
counsel of the ungodly, nor standeth in the way of sinners, nor sitteth in the seat of the scornful.*

2. His reading and thinking. *His delight is in
the law of the Lord; and in his law doth he meditate day
and night.*

3. His fruitfulness. *And he shall be like a tree
planted by the rivers of water, that bringeth forth his fruit
in his season; his leaf also shall not wither; and whatsoever he doeth shall prosper.*

The river is the Holy Spirit; the planting, the
deep abiding life in which, not occasionally but
habitually, we absorb Him. The fruit is not once
in a while, but continual and appropriate to each
changing season.

His life is also prosperous and his spirit fresh,
like the unfading leaf. Such a life must be happy.
Indeed, happiness is a matter of spiritual conditions. Put a sunbeam in a cellar and it must be
bright. Put a nightingale in the darkest midnight,
and it must sing.

I know him . . . that [he] will keep the way of the Lord—Genesis 18:19.

Good wants people whom He can depend upon. He could say of Abraham, *I know him, . . . that the Lord may bring upon Abraham that which he hath spoken of him.* God can be depended upon. He wants us to be just as decided, just as reliable and just as stable. This is what faith means. God is looking for men on whom He can put the weight of all His love and power and faithful promises. When God finds such a soul there is nothing He will not do for him. God's engines are strong enough to pull any weight we attach to them. Unfortunately, the cable which we fasten to the engine is often too weak to hold the weight of our prayer; therefore, God is drilling us, disciplining us and training us that we may achieve stability and certainty in the life of faith. Let us learn our lessons and let us stand fast.

> God has His best things for the few
> Who dare to stand the test;
> God has His second choice for those
> Who will not have His best.

> Give me, O Lord, Thy highest choice,
> Let others take the rest.
> Their good things have no charm
> for me,
> For I have got Thy best.

By this we know that we love the children of God, when we love God, and keep his commandments—1 John 5:2.

"Lovest thou me?" the Master asks of each disciple. He expects our first and highest love for Himself, personally, and He has a right to it. More than all our service, more than all our work to build up a cause, He desires our personal devotion to Him. Mary's gift was precious because it was personal. *Ye have the poor with you always; but me ye have not always* (Mark 14:7), was His tender suggestion of a danger which defeats His purpose—our being more occupied with the work of Christ than with Christ Himself.

We need the love of Christ in order to fit us for His work. Nothing else will give it its true aim and center; nothing else will sustain us amid its pressures.

When Jesus was about to send Simon to take care of His flock, He did not ask Him, "Lovest thou my sheep and my lambs?" He asked, "Lovest thou me?" Mere love for people will not enable us to be true to them; but love for Christ will give us a reflected love for others that will enable us to touch them for Him and to bless them as our direct touch never could.

Now unto him that is able to keep you from falling—Jude 24.

This is a most precious promise. The revised translation is both accurate and suggestive. It is not merely from falling that He wants to keep us, but from even the slightest stumbling.

We are told that Abraham *staggered not at the promise* (Romans 4:20). God wants us to walk so steadily that there will not even be a quiver in the line of His regiments as they face the foe. It is the little stumblings of life that most discourage and hinder us, and most of these stumblings are over trivialities. Satan would much rather knock us down with a feather than with a gun. It is much more to his honor and delight to defeat a child of God by some insignificant matter than by some great temptation.

Beloved, let us be on guard against the banana peels that trip us on our pathway, the little foxes that destroy the vines and the dead flies that spoil a whole vessel of precious ointment. "Trifles make perfection," and as we get farther on in our Christian life, God will hold us much more closely to obedience in things that seem insignificant.

It is I; be not afraid—Mark 6:50.

A little child with a tale of woe on his heart flies to his mother's arms for comfort—intending to tell her the whole story of his trouble. But as soon as that mother takes the child in her arms and expresses her love, the child becomes so occupied with her and the sweetness of her affection that he forgets to tell his story, and in a little while even the memory of the trouble is forgotten. It has just been loved away and the mother has taken its place in the heart of her child.

In this same manner, God comforts us. *It is I; be not afraid* is His reassuring word. The circumstances are not altered, but He Himself comes in their place and satisfies our every need, and we forget all things in His gracious presence as He becomes our all in all.

> I am breathing out my sorrow
> On Thy kind and loving breast;
> Breathing in Thy joy and comfort,
> Breathing in Thy peace and rest.
>
> I am breathing out my longings
> In Thy listening, loving ear;
> I am breathing in Thy answer,
> Stilling every doubt and fear.

Not as I will, but as thou wilt—Matthew 26:39. To will and to do of his good pleasure—Philippians 2:13.

There are two attitudes in which our will should be given to God.

First, we should have the *surrendered will*. This is where we must all begin, by yielding up to God our natural will and having Him possess it.

But next, He wants us to have the *victorious will*. As soon as He receives our will in honest surrender, He wants to put His will into it and make it stronger than ever for Him. It is henceforth no longer our will, but His will. And having yielded to His choice and placed itself under His direction, He wants to put into it all the strength and intensity of His own great will and make us positive, forceful, victorious and unmovable—even as Himself.

Not my will, but thine, be done (Luke 22:42). That is the first step. *Father, I will that they also, whom thou hast given me, be with me* (John 17:24). That is the second attitude. Both are divine; both are right; both are necessary to our right living and successful working for God.

Charity . . . doth not behave itself un-seemly—1 Corinthians 13:5.

The graceful dress of the Hindu woman is fastened upon her person by means of a single knot. The long strip of cloth is wound around her so that it falls in soft folds like a ready-made garment. The end, however, is fastened by a little knot, and the whole thing hangs by that single fastening.

So it is in the spiritual life; our habits of grace can be compared to garments. It is also true that the garment of love, which is the beautiful adorning of the child of God, is entirely fastened by little *nots*.

If you will read First Corinthians chapter 13 with care, you will find that most of the qualities of love are purely negative. *Love . . . envieth* not, *love vaunteth* not *itself, is* not *puffed up, doth* not *behave itself unseemly, seeketh* not *her own, is* not *easily provoked, thinketh no evil.* Here are "nots" enough to hold on our spiritual wardrobe. Here also are reasons enough to explain the failure of so many, and the reason why they walk naked, or with torn garments, allowing others to see their shame. Let us look after the *nots*.

Hold fast till I come—Revelation 2:25.

A Jewish man was asked how it was that his countrymen were so successful in acquiring wealth. "Ah," said he, "we do not make more money than other people, but we keep more." Beloved, let us be on guard this day against spiritual pickpockets and spiritual leakage. Let us *lose not those things which we have wrought.* Let us be sure *we receive a full reward* (2 John 8). As each day comes and goes, let us deposit in the savings bank of eternity its treasures of grace and victory, being conscious that something real and everlasting is being added daily to our eternal fortune.

It may be but a little, but if we can save all that God gives us and pass it on to His keeping, when the end of all things comes, we shall be amazed to see how much the accumulated treasures of a well-spent life have laid up on high. We shall see how much more God has added to them by His glorious investment of the life committed to His keeping.

How the days are passing! How precious these golden hours will seem sometime! God help us to make the most of them now.

Ask, and it shall be given you
—Matthew 7:7.

We must receive, as well as ask. We must take the place of believing and recognize ourselves as in it.

A friend once said to me, "I want to get into the will of God." I answered: "Will you then step into the will of God? And now, are you in the will of God? My question aroused in the man a thought he had not considered. He saw that he had been straining after but not receiving the blessing he sought.

Jesus had said, *Ask, and ye shall receive* (John 16:24). The very strain keeps back the blessing. The strong tension of all your spiritual nature so binds you that you are not open to the blessing which God is waiting to give you. *Whosoever will, let him take the water of life freely* (Revelation 22:17).

> He tells me there is cleansing
> From every secret sin,
> And a great and full salvation
> To keep the heart within
> And I take Him in His fullness,
> With all His glorious grace,
> For He says it is mine by taking,
> And I take just what He says.

Thou shalt be to him instead of God
—Exodus 4:16.

Such was God's promise to Moses, and such the high character that Moses was to assume toward Aaron, his brother. Does it not suggest a high and glorious place that each of us may occupy toward all whom we meet, instead of God?

What a dignity and glory it would give our lives, could we uniformly realize this high calling! What a difference it would make in our actions toward our fellow men! God can always be depended upon. He is without variation. God's Word is unchangeable, and we can trust Him without reserve or question. May we so live that men can trust us, even as they trust God!

Again, God has no needs or wants to be supplied. He is always giving, *rich unto all that call upon him* (Romans 10:12). The glory of His nature is love—unselfish love—and beneficence toward all His creatures. The divine life is a self-forgetting life, a life that has nothing to do but love and bless.

Let us so live, representing our Master here, while He represents us before the Throne on high.

Unto the measure of the stature of the fulness of Christ—Ephesians 4:13.

God loves us so well that He will not permit us to take less than His highest will. Some day we shall thank our faithful Teacher who kept the standard inflexible and then gave us the strength and grace to reach it. We shall thank Him who would not excuse us until we had accomplished all His glorious will.

Let us be inexorable with ourselves. Let us mean exactly what God means, and have no discounts upon His promises or commandments. Let us keep the standard up, and never rest until we reach it. *Let God be true, but every man a liar* (Romans 3:4). Even if we fail a hundred times, let us not accommodate God's ideal to our thinking, let us rather be like the brave ensign who stood in front of his company waving the regimental banner. When the soldiers tried to call him back, he only waved the banner higher and cried, "Don't bring the colors back to the regiment; bring the regiment up to the colors."

> Forward, forward, leave the past
>   behind thee,
> Reaching forth unto the things
>   before;
> All the Land of Promise lies
>   before thee,
> God has greater blessings yet
>   in store.

*As ye have therefore received Christ
Jesus the Lord, so walk ye in him—
Colossians 2:6.*

L et us abide in Him. It is much easier to keep the fire burning than to rekindle it after it has gone out. Let us not have to remove the cinders and ashes from our hearthstones every day and kindle a new flame; but let us keep it burning and never let it expire. Among the ancient Greeks the sacred fire was never allowed to go out. So, in a higher sense, let us keep the heavenly flame aglow upon the altar of our hearts.

It takes much less effort to maintain a good habit than to form it. A true spiritual habit once formed becomes a spontaneous tendency of our being, and we grow into delightful freedom in following it. *Let us go on unto perfection; not laying again the foundation of repentance from dead works* (Hebrews 6:1); *whereto we have already attained, let us walk by the same rule, let us mind the same thing* (Philippians 3:16).

Every spiritual habit begins with difficulty and effort and watchfulness. But if we will only let it get thoroughly established, it will become a channel along which the currents of life will flow with divine spontaneousness and freedom.

*Prove what is that good, and acceptable,
and perfect, will of God—Romans 12:2.*

The water in a steam locomotive may be at any one of three temperatures. It may be cold, although clean and ready for the fire. It may be hot, very hot—hot enough to scald you, almost boiling. Or the water may be just one degree hotter—at the boiling point—pouring out its vapor in clouds of steam, pressing through the valves and driving the mighty pistons that turn the wheels and propel the train.

There are three kinds of Christians. The first we will call cold-water Christians—perhaps better, clean-water Christians.

The second are hot-water Christians. They are almost at the boiling point.

One degree more, and we come to the third class of Christians—the boiling-water Christians. The difference between the latter two is a very slight one. It is simply the removal of one last reservation, the dropping of one "if." Yet it makes all the difference in the world. That one degree changes that engine into a motive power, not now just a machine to be looked at, but a locomotive to go.

It is God which worketh in you
—Philippians 2:13.

God does not have two ways for any of us, but one. Not two things for us to do which we may choose between, but one best and highest choice. It is a blessed thing to find and fill the perfect will of God. It is a blessed thing to have our life laid out and our Christian work adjusted to God's plan.

Much strength is lost by working at a venture. Much spiritual force can be expended in wasted effort and in scattered, indefinite and inconstant attempts at doing good. There is spiritual force and financial strength enough in the hands and hearts of the consecrated Christians of today, if it were only wisely directed and used according to God's plan, to bring about the evangelization of the world in a generation.

Christ has laid down a definite plan of work for His Church, and He expects us to understand it and to work up to it. As we catch His thought and obediently, loyally fulfill it, we shall work with purpose. In so doing we please Him far better than by our thoughtless, reckless and indiscriminate attempts to carry out *our* ideas and compel God to bless *our* work.

That take, and give unto them for me and thee—Matthew 17:27.

There is a beautiful touch of loving thoughtfulness in the account of Christ's miracle at Capernaum in providing the tribute money. After the reference to Peter's interview with the tax collector, the Scriptures add, *when he was come into the house, Jesus prevented him* (17:25); that is, anticipated him, as the old Saxon word means. Jesus arranged for the need before Peter had to speak about it at all and sent him down to the sea to find the piece of gold in the mouth of the fish.

So the Lord is always thinking in advance of our needs. He loves to save us from embarrassment. He anticipates and cares by laying up His loving acts and providing before the emergency comes.

Then with exquisite tenderness the Master adds: *That take, and give to them for me and thee.* He puts Himself first in the embarrassing need and bears the heavy end of the burden for His distressed and suffering child. He makes our cares His cares, our sorrows His sorrows, our shame His shame. He is able to be *touched with the feeling of our infirmities* (Hebrews 4:15).

Prove me now herewith—Malachi 3:10.

I once heard an old man say something that I have never forgotten. "When God tests you it is a good time for you to test Him by putting His promises to the proof. Claim from Him just as much as your trials have made necessary."

There are two ways of getting out of a trial. One is simply to try to get rid of the trial, and be thankful when it is over. The other is to recognize the trial as a challenge from God to claim a larger blessing than we have ever had. We should greet it with delight as an opportunity of obtaining a larger measure of divine grace.

Thus even the adversary becomes an auxiliary, and the things that seem to be against us turn out to be for the furtherance of our way. Surely, we are to be *more than conquerors through him who loved us* (Romans 8:37).

> Blessed Rose of Sharon
> Breathe upon our heart,
> Fill us with Thy fragrance,
> Keep us as Thou art.
> Then Thy life will make us
> Holy and complete;
> In Thy grace triumphant,
> In Thy sweetness, sweet.

Ye know not what manner of spirit ye are of—Luke 9:55.

Someone has said that the most spiritual people are the easiest to get along with. When one has a little of the Holy Spirit it is like "a little learning, a dangerous thing." But a full baptism of the Holy Spirit and a really disciplined, established and tested spiritual life makes one simple, tender, tolerant, considerate and childlike.

James and John, in their early zeal, wanted to call down fire from heaven on the Samaritans. But John, the aged, allowed Demetrius to exclude him from the church, and, with the patience of Jesus, suffered on Patmos for the kingdom. And aged Paul was willing to take back even Mark, whom he had refused as a companion in his early ministry and to acknowledge that he was profitable to him for the ministry.

> I want the love that cannot help
>   but love;
> Loving, like God, for very sake of love.
> A spring so full that it must overflow,
> A fountain flowing from the
>   throne above.

Now abideth faith, hope, [love]; but the greatest of these is [love] (1 Corinthians 13:13).

Pray without ceasing
—1 Thessalonians 5:17.

An important help in the life of prayer is the habit of bringing *everything* to God, moment by moment, as it comes to us in life. This may become a habit the same way all habits are formed: repeated and constantly attended, moment by moment, until that which is at first an act of will becomes spontaneous and second nature.

If we will watch our lives, we shall find that God meets the things that we commit to Him in prayer with special blessing. He often allows the best things that we have not committed to Him to be ineffectual, simply to remind us of our dependence upon Him for everything. It is very gracious and thoughtful of God to compel us gently to remember Him. He would hold us so close to Himself that we cannot get away for a single minute from His all-sustaining arm. *In every thing . . . let your requests be made known unto God* (Philippians 4:6).

> Let us bring our least petitions,
> Like the incense beaten small,
> All our cares, complaints, conditions
> Jesus loves to bear them all.

....

His wife hath made herself ready
—Revelation 19:7.

There is danger of becoming morbid even in preparing for the Lord's coming. I remember a time when I determined to devote myself to a month of waiting upon the Lord for a baptism of the Holy Ghost. Before the end of the month the Lord had shaken me out of the seclusion and compelled me to go out and carry His message to others. As I went He met me in my service to Him.

There is a musty, monkish way of seeking a blessing. There is also a wholesome, practical holiness which finds us in the company of the Lord Himself, not only in the closet and on the mountaintop of prayer but among publicans and sinners and in the practical duties of life.

The practical preparation for the Lord's coming consists first of fully entering into fellowship with Him in our own spiritual lives, letting Him not only cleanse us, but perfect us in all the finer touches of the Spirit's deeper work. Following that it will mean getting out of ourselves and living for the benefit of others and the preparation of the world for His appearing.

··

I knew a man in Christ
—2 Corinthians 12:2.

It is a great deliverance to lose one's self. There is no heavier millstone than self-consciousness. It is so easy to become introverted and coiled around ourselves in our spiritual consciousness. There is nothing that is so easy to fasten onto as our misery: there is nothing that is more apt to produce self-consciousness than suffering. Then it becomes almost a settled habit to hold onto our burden and pray it unceasingly into the very face of God until even our prayer saturates us with our own misery. Rather, we should ask for power to drop ourselves altogether and leave ourselves in His loving hands and know that we are free. Then we may rise into the blessed liberty of His higher thoughts and will and demonstrate His love and care for others.

The very act of letting go of ourselves lifts us into a higher place and relieves us from the thing that is hurting. This habit of prayer for others, and especially for the world, brings its own recompense and leaves upon our hearts a blessing, like the fertility which the Nile deposits upon the soil of Egypt as it flows through to its ultimate goal.

Freely ye have received, freely give
—Matthew 10:8.

When God does anything marked and special for our souls or bodies, He intends it as a sacred trust for us to communicate to others. *Freely ye have received, freely give.*

It has pleased the Master in these closing days of His dispensation of grace to reveal Himself in peculiar blessing to the hearts of His chosen disciples in all parts of the Christian church. But this is intended to be communicated to a still wider circle. Every one of us who has been brought into these intimate relations with God becomes a trustee or witness for these higher truths to everyone we can influence.

If God has revealed Himself to us as our Sanctifier, it is that we may help others to know Him as a Sanctifier.

If He has become our Healer, it is because there are sick and suffering people to whom we can bring some blessing.

In like manner, if the hope of the Lord's coming has become precious to us, it would be worse than ingratitude for us to hide our testimony to this truth and hold it only for our own personal comfort.

Hold fast that which is good
—1 Thessalonians 5:21.

It is good to be able to receive new truth and blessing without sacrificing the truths already proved or abandoning foundations already laid.

Some persons are always laying the foundations, until, finally, they appear like a number of abandoned sites and half-constructed buildings. Nothing is ever brought to completion.

If today you are abandoning for some new truth the things that a year ago you counted most precious and believed to be divinely true, this should be sufficient evidence that a year from now you will probably abandon your present convictions for the next new light that comes to you.

God wants to continually add to us, to develop us, to enlarge us, to teach us more and more but always building on what He has already taught us and what He has established in our lives.

While we are to *prove all things*, let us *hold fast that which is good*, and *whereto we have already attained, let us walk by the same rule, let us mind the same thing* (Philippians 3:16).

I called him alone, and blessed him
—Isaiah 51:2.

R aising rice in the Orient is a beautiful process. The rice is sown on a morass of mud and water ploughed up by great buffaloes. After a few weeks the pale green shoots spring up, appearing above the water. The seed has been sown very thickly and the plants are clustered together in great numbers. The farmer can pull up a score in a single handful. At that point the shoots are ready for transplanting.

So God first plants us and lets us grow very close to some of His children. We may be in great clusters in the nursery or the hothouse. But when we reach a certain stage we must be transplanted or come to nothing. God calls us out by His Spirit and Providence into situations where we have to lean directly on Him. He puts upon us a weight of responsibility so great that we are thrown upon the limitless resources of His grace and have an opportunity to develop.

Blessed is the man that trusteth in the Lord, and whose hope the Lord is. For he shall be as a tree planted by the waters, and that spreadeth out her roots by the river (Jeremiah 17:7-8).

This one thing I do—Philippians 3:13.

One of Satan's favorite employees is the switchman. He likes nothing better than to sidetrack one of God's express trains sent on some blessed mission and filled with the fire of a holy purpose.

Something will come up in the pathway of the earnest man to attract his attention and occupy his strength and thought. Sometimes it is a little irritation or provocation. Sometimes it is some petty grievance he stops to pursue or adjust. Sometimes it is somebody else's business in which he becomes interested, and he feels bound to rectify. Before he knows it, he is absorbed in many distracting cares and interests that turn him aside from the great purpose of his life.

Perhaps he does not do much harm, but he has missed his connection. He has left the main line.

Let all these things alone. Let grievances come and go, but press forward steadily and irresistibly, crying as you speed toward the goal, *This one thing I do!*

*That my joy might remain in you, and
that your joy might be full—John 15:11.*

There is a joy that springs spontaneously in
the heart without any external or even
rational cause. It is like an artesian fountain. It
rejoices because it cannot help it. It is the glory
of God; it is the heart of Christ; it is the joy divine
of which He says, *These things have I spoken unto
you, that my joy might remain in you, and that your joy
might be full* (John 15:11). And your joy no man
can take from you. Those who possess this fountain are not discouraged by surrounding circumstances. Rather, they are often surprised at the
deep, sweet gladness that comes without appar-
ent cause—a joy that frequently is strongest
when everything in their condition and circumstances would tend to fill them with sorrow and
depression.

It is the nightingale in the heart that sings at
night because it is its nature to sing.

It is the glorified and incorruptible joy that
belongs with heaven and anticipates already the
everlasting song. Lord, give us Thy joy under all
circumstances this day, and let our full hearts
overflow in blessing to others.

Send portions unto them for
whom nothing is prepared
—Nehemiah 8:10.

Nehemiah gives us a graphic picture concerning what took place during the celebration of their glorious Feast of Tabernacles. *Go your way, eat the fat, and drink the sweet, and send portions to them for whom nothing is prepared: . . . neither be ye sorry; for the joy of the Lord is your strength.*

How many there are on every side for whom nothing is prepared! Let us find some sad and needy heart whom there is no one else to think of or care for. Let us pray for someone who has none to pray for him. Let us be like Him who, one Christmas Day, came to a world that would not appreciate Him, to be rejected and finally murdered.

Let us not be afraid to know something even of the love that is unrequited and is thrown away on the unworthy. That is the love of Christ, and God has for such love a rich recompense.

How Christ must weep over the selfishness that meets Him from those for whom He died!

Cast down, but not destroyed
—2 Corinthians 4:9.

How did God bring about the miracle of the Red Sea? By shutting His people in on every side so that there was no way out but the divine way. The Egyptians were behind them, the sea was in front of them, the mountains were on both sides of them. There was no escape but from above.

Someone has said that the devil can wall us in, but he cannot roof us over. We can always get out at the top. Our difficulties are but God's challenges, and many times He makes them so hard that we must get above them or go under.

In the Providence of God, such an hour furnishes us with the highest possibilities for faith. We are pushed by the very emergency into God's best.

Beloved, this is God's hour. If you will rise to meet it you will get such a hold upon Him that you will never be in extremities again; or if you are, you will learn to call them not extremities, but opportunities. Like Jacob, you will go forth from that night at Peniel, no longer Jacob, but victorious Israel. Let us bring to Him our need and prove Him true.

Jesus, who of God is made unto us wisdom, and righteousness, and sanctification, and redemption—1 Corinthians 1:30.

More and more we are realizing the supreme importance of getting the right conception of sanctification—not as a blessing but as a personal union with the personal Savior and the indwelling Holy Spirit.

Thousands of people get stranded after they have embarked on the great voyage of holiness. They find themselves failing and falling and are astonished and perplexed. They conclude that they must have been mistaken in their experience. So they make a new attempt at the same thing and again fall. At last, worn out with their efforts, they conclude that the experience is a delusion, or at least that it was never intended for them. Then they fall back into the old way, and their last state is worse than their first.

What people need today to satisfy their deep hunger and to give them a permanent and divine experience is to know not sanctification as a state but Christ as a living person who is waiting to enter the heart that is willing to receive Him.

A . . . well of water springing up
—John 4:14.

In the life overflowing in service for others we find God's deep fountain spilling over the spring to find outlet in rivers of living water that bless and save the world around us. It is beautiful to notice that as the blessing grows unselfish it grows larger. The water in the heart is only a well, but when reaching out to the needs of others it is not only a river but a delta of many rivers overflowing in majestic blessing. This overflowing love is connected with the person and work of the Holy Spirit who was poured out upon the disciples after Jesus was glorified.

This is the true secret of power for service— the heart filled and satisfied with Jesus and so baptized with the Holy Spirit that it is impelled by the fullness of its joy and love to impart to others what it has so abundantly received. And yet each new ministry only makes room for a new filling and a deeper receiving of the life which grows by giving.

> Letting go is twice possessing.
> Would you double every blessing?
> Pass it on.

*But whosoever will be great among you,
let him be your minister; and whosoever
will be chief among you, let him be your
servant—Matthew 20:26-27.*

The first word here used for service is
diakanos, which means minister to others
in any usual way or work. The word *doulos,* however, means a bondservant, and the Lord here
plainly teaches us that this is the highest form of
service.

Christ made Himself the servant of all, and he
who would come nearest to Him and stand closest to Him at last must likewise learn the spirit
of the ministry that has utterly renounced selfish
rights and claims forever.

It is quite possible for us to be entirely loyal to
the Lord Jesus, and yet for His sake to be servants
and under the authority of those who are over us
in the Lord.

The *doulos* spirit is the spirit of self-renunciation and glad submission to proper authority—service utterly disinterested, yielding its
own preferences and interests unreservedly for
the glory of the Master and the sake of our brethren. Lord, clothe us with such humility and make
us wholly Thine.

He went out, not knowing whither he went—Hebrews 11:8.

This is true faith. When we can see, it is not faith but reasoning. In crossing the Atlantic by ship, I observed this very principle of faith. We could see no path upon the water or sign of the shore. And yet day by day the helmsman was in a path as exactly as if he had been following a great chalk line upon the sea. And when we came within 20 miles of land he knew where we were as surely as if he had seen it all 3,000 miles ahead.

How had we measured and marked our course? Day by day our captain had taken his instruments, and looking up to the sky had fixed his course by the sun. He was sailing by the heavenly lights, not the earthly lights. So faith looks up and sails on, by God's great Sun, not seeing one shoreline or earthly lighthouse or path upon the way. Often our steps seem to lead into utter uncertainty or even darkness and disaster. But He opens the way, making our midnight hours the very gates of day.

Let us go forth this day, not knowing, yet trusting.

Lo, I am with you alway
—Matthew 28:20.

This living Christ is not the person who *was*, but the person who *still is* your living Lord.

At Preston Pans, near Edinburgh, I looked on the field where, long ago, armies had been engaged in contest. In the crisis of the battle the chieftain fell wounded. When they saw their leader's form go down, his men were about to shrink away from the field. Their strong hands held the claymore with trembling grip, and they faltered for a moment. Then the old chieftain rallied strength enough to rise on his elbow and cry: "I am not dead, my children, I am only watching you—to see my clansmen do their duty."

And so from the other side of Calvary our Savior is speaking. We cannot see Him, but He says, *Lo, I am with you alway, even unto the end of the world* (Matthew 28:20). Notice how He puts it: "I am"—an uninterrupted and continuous presence. Not "I will be," but the guarantee of an unbroken presence to remain with us forever.

> Soon the conflict shall be done,
> Soon the battle shall be won;
> Soon shall wave the victor's palm,
> Soon shall sing the eternal psalm.
> Then our joyful song shall be,
> I have overcome through Thee.

Rest in the Lord—Psalm 38.

In the old creation, the week began with work and ended with Sabbath rest. The resurrection week begins with the first day—first rest, then labor.

So we must first cease from our own works as God did from His, and enter into His rest. And then, with rested hearts, we will work His works with effectual power.

But why *labor to enter into rest?* See that sailing craft—how restfully it glides over the waters, its canvas swelling with the wind and borne without an effort! And yet, look at that man at the helm. See how firmly he holds the rudder, bearing against the wind, and holding her steady to her position. Let him for a moment relax his steady hold and the vessel will fall listlessly along the wind. The sails will flap, the waves will toss the craft at their will, and all rest and power will have gone. It is the fixed helm that brings the steadying power of the wind. And so He has said, *Thou wilt keep him in perfect peace, whose mind is stayed on thee: because he trusteth in thee* (Isaiah 26:3). The steady will and stayed heart are ours. The keeping is the Lord's. So let us labor to enter and abide in His rest.

Praying always . . . for all saints
—Ephesians 6:18.

W hat a priceless bit of counsel! Stop praying so much for yourself; begin to ask
unselfish things, and see if God will not give you
faith. See how much easier it will be to believe
for another than for your own concerns.

Try the effect of praying for the world, for
definite things, for difficult things, for glorious
things, for things that will honor Christ and save
mankind. After you have received a few wonderful answers to prayer in this direction, see
if you will not feel stronger to touch your own
little burden with a divine faith and then go back
again to the high place of unselfish prayer for
others.

Have you ever learned the beautiful art of letting God take care of you and giving all your
thought and strength to pray for others and for
the kingdom of God? It will relieve you of a
thousand cares. It will lift you up into a noble
and lofty sphere and teach you to live and love
like God. Lord, save us from our selfish prayers;
give us the faith that works through love and
the heart of Christ for a perishing world.

Faithful in that which is least
—Luke 16:10.

The man who missed his opportunity and met the doom of the faithless servant was not the man with five talents, or the man with two, but the man who had only one. The people who are in danger of missing life's great meaning are the people of ordinary capacity and opportunity who say to themselves, *There is so little I can do that I will not try to do anything.*

One of the finest windows in Europe was made from the remnants an apprentice boy collected from the cuttings of his master's great work. The sweepings of the British mint are worth millions. The little pivots on which the works of a watch turn are so important that they actually are made of jewels.

God places a solemn value on a single talent. He puts a large responsibility on the humble workers and persons who would try to hide behind the insignificance of trifling opportunities. Our littleness will not excuse us in the reckoning day.

> Talk not of talents; what hast
>   thou to do?
> Thou hast sufficient, whether
>   five or two.
> Talk not of talents; is thy
>   duty done?
> This brings the blessing whether
>   ten or one.

[We are not] sufficient of our-
selves to think any thing as of our-
selves—2 Corinthians 3:5.

Not sufficient—all sufficient. These two expressions are the complement of each other. Together they are the key to an effective Christian life.

The discovery and full conviction of our utter helplessness is the constant condition for spiritual supply. The aim of the Old Testament, there-fore, is ever to show man's failure; that of the New, to reveal Christ's sufficiency. He has all things for us, but we cannot receive them until we admit that we have nothing.

The very essence, therefore, of Christian per-fection is the constant renunciation of our own perfection and the continual acceptance of Christ's righteousness. And as we receive deeper views of our nothingness and evil, it prompts us to claim more of His rich grace. But it is possible fully to realize our insufficiency and yet not take a firm hold of His "all things." This, too, must be done with a faith that will not accept less than all. The prophet was angry because the king of Israel struck the arrows upon the ground only three times. Had he done so five or six times, he could have had all (see 2 Kings 13:14-19). So let us meet God's full requirement. In humility let us receive His greatness and grace.

None of these things move me
—Acts 20:24.

The best evidence of God's presence is the devil's growl. So once wrote Charles H. Spurgeon in *The Sword and the Trowel.* That little sentence has helped many a tried and tired child of God to stand fast and even rejoice under the fiercest attacks of the foe.

We read in the book of Second Samuel that the moment David was crowned at Hebron, "All the Philistines came up to seek David." And the moment we get anything from the Lord worth contending for, the devil comes to seek us.

When the enemy meets us at the threshold of any great work for God, let us accept it as "a token of salvation" and claim double blessing, victory and power. Power is developed by resistance. The cannon carries twice as far because the exploding power has to find its way through resistance. In the powerhouse, electricity is produced by the magnetic resistance of the revolving armature. Even so we shall find some day that Satan has been one of God's agencies of blessing.

*I am crucified with Christ: never-
theless I live—Galatians 2:20.*

The Christ life is in harmony with our
nature. The other day I was asked by a
thoughtful, intelligent woman—one not a Christian, but who had the deepest hunger for that
which is right—"How can Christ enter us and
we not lose our individuality? This experience
will destroy our personality; it violates our
responsibility as individuals."

My response was, "Your personality is incomplete without Christ. Christ was made for you,
and you were made for Christ, and until you
meet Him you are not complete. He needs you as
you need Him.

"Suppose," I continued, "that gas jet should
say, 'If I take this fire in, the gas coursing
through me will lose its individuality.' Oh, no;
it is only when the fire comes in that the gas ful-
fills its purpose for being.

"Suppose the snowflake should say, 'What
shall I do? If I drop on the ground I shall lose my
individuality.' But it falls and is absorbed by the
soil, and with the coming spring the snowflakes
are seen in the primroses and daisies."

Let us lose ourselves and rise to a new life in
Christ.

Strengthened with all might . . .
unto all patience—Colossians 1:11.

The apostle Paul prays for the Colossians to be *strengthened with all might, according to his glorious power, unto all patience and longsuffering with joyfulness.* It is one thing to endure and show the strain on every muscle of your face, seeming to say with every wrinkle, "Why doesn't someone sympathize with me?" It is another thing to endure the cross, *despising the shame* for the joy set before us.

There are some trees in the garden of the Lord which *shall not see when heat cometh, but her leaf shall be green; and shall not be careful in the year of drought, neither shall cease from yielding fruit* (Jeremiah 17:8). Let us set our faces toward the sun rising, and use the clouds that come to make rainbows.

Not much longer shall we have glorious opportunity to rejoice in tribulation and learn patience. In heaven we shall have nothing to teach us long-suffering. If we do not learn it here, we shall be without our brightest crown forever and wish ourselves back for a little while in the very circumstances of which we are now trying so hard to rid ourselves.

*But seek ye first the kingdom of God,
and his righteousness; and all these things
shall be added unto you—Matthew 6:33.*

For every heart that is seeking anything from the Lord this is a good watchword. That very thing, or the desire for it, may unconsciously separate us from the Lord or at least from the singleness of our purpose toward Him. The thing we desire may be a right thing, but we may desire it in a distrustful and selfish spirit. Let us commit it to Him and believe for it; but let us, at the same time, keep our purpose fixed on His will and glory.

Let us claim even His promised blessings, not for themselves or ourselves, but for Him. Then shall it be true, *Delight thyself also in the Lord; and he shall give thee the desires of thine heart* (Psalm 37:4). All other things but Himself God will "add." But they must always be added, never first. Then shall we be able to believe for them without doubt, when we claim them for Him and not for ourselves. It is only when *we are Christ's* that *all things are ours.*

Lord, help me this day to seek Thee first, and be more desirous to please Thee and have Thy will than to possess any other blessing.

Thy prayers . . . are come up for a memorial before God—Acts 10:4.

What a beautiful expression the angel used to Cornelius, *Thy prayers are come up for a memorial.* It would almost seem as if supplications of years had accumulated before the Throne, and at last the answer broke in blessings on the head of Cornelius, even as the accumulated evaporation of months bursts in floods of rain upon the parched ground.

God is represented as treasuring the prayers of His saints in vials; they are described as sweet odors. They are placed like fragrant flowers in the chambers of the king and kept in constant remembrance before Him. Later they are said to be poured out upon the earth; and lo, there are voices, and thunderings and great providential movements fulfilling God's purposes for His kingdom.

We are called "the Lord's remembrancers," and are commanded to give Him no rest, day or night, but to crowd the heavens with our petitions. And in due time the answer will come with its accumulated blessings.

Not a whisper of true prayer is ever lost. The longer it waits, the larger it becomes.

....

He shall baptize you . . . with fire
—Matthew 3:11.

Fire is strangely intense and intrinsic. It goes into the very substance of things. It somehow blends with every particle of the thing it touches.

There are the severe trials that come to minds more sensitive—to minds that have more points of contact with what hurts. The higher the nature, the higher the joy and the greater the avenues of pain that come.

And then there are deeper trials that come as we pass into the hands of God, as we pass from the physical and intellectual into the spiritual. When they first come, we shrink back from their unnatural and fearful breath. We say, "Oh, this cannot be from the hand of a loving Father! This cannot be necessary to me."

And then come the pains and sufferings from God's own hand, when He sits as a refiner and purifier of silver, when He lets it burn until it seems that we must be burned to ashes.

But we can only obtain the victory through faith. The moment we cease to fear the fire, that moment it ceases to harm us. He says, *Neither shall the flame kindle upon thee* (Isaiah 43:2).

*Be strong in the grace that is in
Christ Jesus—2 Timothy 2:1.*

How may we enjoy this day? This enjoyment will never come by trying to be happy, and yet there are conditions which, if met, will produce real joy.

1.   Be right with God, for *gladness [is sown] for the upright in heart* (Psalm 97:11). It is His joy that remains in us that makes our joy full.

2.   Forget yourself and live for others, for *It is more blessed to give than to receive* (Acts 20:35).

3.   When you cannot rejoice in feelings, circumstances or conditions, *rejoice in the Lord* (Philippians 4:4), and *count it all joy when ye fall into divers temptations* (James 1:2).

4.   Finally, obey the Lord and be faithful to your trust, and again and again His blessed Spirit will whisper to your heart, *Well done, thou good and faithful servant, . . . enter thou into the joy of thy lord* (Matthew 25:21).

> Not enjoyment and not sorrow
> Is our destined end or way,
> But to act that each tomorrow
> Finds us farther than today.
>
> Let us then be up and doing
> With a heart for any fate,
> Still achieving, still pursuing,
> Learn to labor and to wait.

> *From "A Psalm of Life"*
> *Henry Wadsworth Longfellow*

*We will give ourselves continually
to prayer—Acts 6:4.*

In the consecrated believer the Holy Spirit is preeminently a Spirit of prayer. If our whole being is committed to Him and our thoughts are under His control, He will occupy every moment in communion. We shall bring everything to Him as it comes, and pray it out in our spiritual consciousness before we act it out in our lives. We shall, therefore, find ourselves taking up the burdens of life and praying them out in a wordless prayer which we ourselves often cannot understand, but which is simply the unfolding of His thought and will within us. This will be followed by the unfolding of His providence concerning us.

Unfaithfulness and disobedience to the faintest whisper of His will will often hinder some blessing which He meant for us. After a while, we may become so dull and negligent that He will not be able to trust us with His whispers, and we shall stumble on in the darkness and miss His highest thoughts.

Lord, teach us to pray in the Spirit, to pray without ceasing, and to lose nothing of Thy will.

Your life is hid—Colossians 3:3.

Some Christians rise in larger proportion than is becoming. They can tell, and others can tell, how many souls they bring to Christ. Their labor seems to crystallize and become its own memorial.

Other Christians seem to blend so completely with their fellow workers that their individuality can scarcely be traced. Yet, this is the most Christlike ministry of all, for even the Master Himself does not appear in the work of the Church except as her hidden Life and ascended Head, and the Holy Spirit is lost in the vessels that He uses.

The vine does not bear the fruit, it is the little branches which bear all the clusters and seem to have all the honor of the vintage. Even the sap is unseen in its ceaseless flow. And so, the nearer we come to Christ the more we are willing to lose sight of ourselves, and let others be more prominent. We uphold them by the silent ministry of our love and prayer.

Lord, let me be like the veiled seraphim before the throne, who cover their faces and their feet, and hide themselves and their service while they fly to obey Thee.

Christ in you—Colossians 1:27.

How great the difference between the old and the new way of deliverance! One touch of Christ is worth a lifetime of struggling.

A sufferer in a hospital was in danger of losing his sight from a small piece of broken needle that had entered his eye. Operation after operation had only irritated it and driven the foreign substance farther still into the delicate parts of the sensitive organ.

Finally, a skillful young physician thought of a new expedient. He came one day without lancet and probes, holding only a small but powerful magnet which he placed before the wounded eye. Immediately the piece of steel began to move toward the powerful attraction; soon it flew up to meet it and left the suffering eye completely relieved without an effort or laceration.

It was as simple as it was wonderful. By a single touch of power the eye was saved and a dangerous trouble completely cured. In the same way, God delivers us by the simple attraction of Christ's life and power.

As much as in me is, I am ready
—Romans 1:15.

Be earnest. Intense earnestness, a whole heart for Christ, the passion sign of the cross, the enthusiasm of our whole being for our Master and humanity—this is what the Lord expects. This is what His cross deserves, this is what the world needs and this is what the age has a right to look for.

Everything around us is intensely alive. Life is earnest, death is earnest, sin is earnest, man is earnest, business is earnest, knowledge is earnest, the age is earnest. God forgive us if we are lax in the white heat of this crisis time.

Oh, for the baptism of fire! Oh, for the living coal upon the burning lips of love! Oh, for men and women God-possessed and self-surrendered, grasping God's great idea and pressing forward *toward the mark for the prize of the high calling of God in Christ Jesus* (Philippians 3:14).

> All the world for Jesus
> My prayer shall be,
> And my watchword ever,
> Himself for me.
>
> All the world for Jesus,
> Lord, quickly come,
> Bring Thy promised kingdom,
> And take us home.

Fear thou not; for I am with thee
—Isaiah 41:10.

S atan is continually trying to weaken our faith by fear. He is a great metaphysician and knows the paralyzing effect of fear—the great enemy of faith. If he can cause us to fear, he will stop us from trusting and hinder the very blessing we need. Job found the peril of fear and gives us the sorrowful testimony *I feared a fear, and it came upon me* (Job 3:25, margin).

Fear is born of Satan, and if we would only take time to think a moment we would see that everything Satan says is founded upon a falsehood. He is the father of lies. Even his fears are falsehoods and his terrors ought to serve as encouragements.

When Satan tells you, therefore, that some ill is going to come, you may quietly look in his face and tell him he is a liar. Instead of ill, goodness and mercy shall follow you all the days of your life. And then turn to your blessed Lord and say, *What time I am afraid, I will trust in thee* (Psalm 56:3). Every fear is distrust, and trust is the remedy for fear.

Be not dismayed; for I am thy God
—Isaiah 41:10.

How tenderly God soothes our fears! How sweetly He says in the introductory verse, *Fear thou not; for I am with thee: be not dismayed; for I am thy God: . . . I will uphold thee with the right hand of my righteousness.* And yet again, still with tender thoughtfulness, *I the Lord thy God will hold thy right hand, saying unto thee, Fear not; I will help thee* (Isaiah 41:13). He does not say it only once, but He keeps holding our right hand and repeating such promises.

The blessed Lord condensed it all into one single message of eternal comfort spoken to the disciples on the Sea of Galilee, *It is I; be not afraid. He* is the antidote to fear; *He* is the remedy for trouble; *He* is the substance and the sum of deliverance. We should, therefore, rise above fear. Let us keep our eyes fastened upon Him; let us abide continually in Him; let us be content with Him.

Let us cling closely to Him and cry, *Therefore will not we fear, though the earth be removed, and though the mountains be carried into the midst of the sea* (Psalm 46:2).

He that is entered into his rest, he also hath ceased from his own works, as God did from his—Hebrews 4:10.

What a rest it would be to many of us if we could exchange burdens with Christ and so utterly and irreversibly transfer to Him all our cares and needs that we would no longer feel responsible for them. We would have the assurance that He has undertaken all the care, and that He prays, labors and suffers only for us and our interests.

In reality, this is what He invites us to do. *Come unto me,* He says, *all ye that labour and are heavy laden, and I will give you rest,* and then He adds, *Take my yoke upon you, and learn of me* (Matthew 11:28-29). He takes our yoke and we take His, and we find it a thousand times easier to carry one of His burdens than to carry our own.

How much more delightful it is to spend an hour in supplication for another than five minutes in pleading for ourselves. Are we not weary of carrying our wretched loads?

> 'Twas for this His mercy sought you,
> And to all His fullness brought you,
> By the precious blood that bought you,
> Pass it on.

*For to me to live is Christ, and to
die is gain—Philippians 1:21.*

The secret of a sound body is a sound heart,
and the prayer of the Holy Spirit for us is
that we may *prosper and be in health, even as [our]
soul prospereth* (3 John 2).

We find Paul in his Letter to the Philippians
expressing a sublime and holy indifference to the
question of life or death. Indeed, he is in a real
strait, whether preferring *to depart, and to be with
Christ* (1:23), or to remain in the flesh.

He would prefer the former, but the latter
would likewise be a joyful service. His only
object in wanting to live was to be a blessing: *To
abide in the flesh is more needful for you* (1:24).

Having reached this state of heart, he rises
quickly to the victorious faith necessary to claim
perfect strength and health. Because it is more
beneficial to them that he remain in the flesh, he
adds, *I know that I shall abide and continue with you all
for your furtherance and joy of faith* (1:25).

Lord, help me today to count not *my life dear
unto myself, so that I might finish my course with joy,
and the ministry, which I have received of the Lord
Jesus* (Acts 20:24).

··

Sin shall not have dominion over you: for ye are not under the law, but under grace —Romans 6:14.

The secret of Moses' failures was this: *The law made nothing perfect, but the bringing in of a better hope did* (Hebrews 7:19). And this was why his life work also came short of full realization. He saw but did not enter Canaan. The founder of the law had to be its victim, and his life and death well demonstrate the inability of the law to lead any man into the Promised Land. Realizing that Moses lost his inheritance for so slight a fault makes all the more emphatic the solemn sentence of the law. *Cursed is every one that continueth not in all things which are written in the book of the law to do them* (Galatians 3:10).

But to the glory of the grace of God we can add that what the law could not do for Moses the gospel did; and he who could not pass over the Jordan under the old dispensation is seen on the very heights of Hermon with the Son of man, sharing His transfiguration glory and talking of that death on Calvary to which he owed his glorious destiny.

That same grace we have inherited under the gospel of Jesus Christ.

....

I am the vine, ye are the branches
—*John 15:5.*

H ow can I take Christ as my Sanctifier or
Healer? That is a question that we are constantly asked.

It is necessary first of all that we get into the
posture of faith. This has to be done by a definite
and voluntary act, and then maintained by a
uniform habit. It is just the same as the planting
of a tree. You must put it in the soil by a definite
act, and then you must let it stay there and remain settled in the ground until the little roots
have time to fix themselves and begin to draw
the sustenance from the soil.

There are two stages: the definite planting and
then the habitual absorbing of moisture and
nourishment from the ground. The root fibers
must rest until they reach out their spongy pores
and drink in the nutriment of the earth. After the
habit is established, then by a certain uniform
law the plant draws its life from the ground
without an effort, and it is just as natural for
it to grow as it is for us to breathe.

Lord, help me this day to abide in Thee, and to
grow into the habit of drawing all my life from
Yours so that it shall be true for me, *in* [*you*]
[*I*] *live, and move, and have* [*my*] *being*
(Acts 17:28).

Make you perfect in every good work
—Hebrews 13:21.

The prayer at the close of the Letter to the Hebrews is beautiful: *Now the God of peace, that brought again from the dead our Lord Jesus, that great shepherd of the sheep, through the blood of the everlasting covenant, make you perfect in every good work to do his will* (Hebrews 13:20-21). The phrase "make you perfect in every good work" literally means, "adjust you in every good work."

It is a great thing to be adjusted—adjusted to our surroundings and circumstances rather than trying to have them adjusted to us. Adjusted to the people we are thrown with. Adjusted to the work God has for us, not trying to get God to help *us* to do *our* work. Adjusted to fulfill the very will and plan of God for us in our whole life. This is the secret of rest, power and freedom in every spiritual endeavor.

> Oh, fill me with Thy fullness, Lord.
> Until my very heart o'erflow
> In kindling thought and glowing word,
> Thy love to tell, Thy praise to show.
>
> Oh, use me, Lord, use even me,
> Just as Thou wilt, and when,
>   and where;
> Until Thy blessed face I see,
> Thy rest, Thy joy, Thy glory share.

Stablish, strengthen, settle you
—1 Peter 5:10.

In taking Christ in any new relationship, we must first have sufficient intellectual light to satisfy our minds that we are entitled to stand in this relationship. The shadow of a question here will wreck our confidence. Then, having seen this, we must make the committal, the choice. That commitment must be just as definite as the planting of a tree in the soil, or the bride who presents herself at the marriage altar. It must be once for all, without reserve, without recall.

Then there is a season of establishing, settling and testing, during which we must stay put until the new relationship gets so fixed as to become a permanent habit. For example, when the surgeon sets the broken arm he puts it in splints to keep it from moving until the bone knits. So God has His spiritual splints that He wants to put upon His children to keep them quiet and unmoving until they pass the first stage of faith.

It may not be easy, *but the God of all grace, who hath called you unto his eternal glory by Christ Jesus, after that ye have suffered a while, [will]* . . . *stablish, strengthen, settle you.*

Count it all joy—James 1:2.

W e do not always feel joyful, but we are
to count it all joy. The word "reckon" is
one of the key words of Scripture. It is the same
word used about our death to self (Romans 6:11).
We do not feel dead. We are painfully conscious
of something that would gladly return to life.
But we are to treat ourselves as dead and neither
fear nor obey the old nature.

So we are to reckon the thing that comes as a
blessing. We are determined to rejoice, to say,
*my heart is fixed, O God, my heart is fixed: I will sing
and give praise* (Psalm 57:7). This rejoicing by faith
will soon become a habit and will bring continually the spirit of gladness and the spontaneous
overflow of praise.

Then, *although the fig tree shall not blossom, neither
shall fruit be in the vines; the labor of the olive
shall fail, and the fields shall yield no meat; the flock
shall be cut off from the fold, and there shall be no herd
in the stalls: yet I will rejoice in the Lord, I will joy in
the God of my salvation* (Habakkuk 3:17).

> Peace, perfect peace, with sorrows
>   surging 'round?
> On Jesus' bosom naught but calm
>   is found.
> Peace, perfect peace, our future
>   all unknown?
> Jesus we know, and He is on
>   the throne.

Count it all joy when ye fall into divers temptations—John 1:2-4.

The battle does us good. The conflict educates us, strengthens us, establishes us. It is necessary that we be grounded and settled and finally approved and rewarded.

One of the best results of temptation is that it shows us what is in our hearts. Until temptation comes, we feel strong and self-confident; but when the keen edge of the adversary's weapons have pierced our souls, we have more sympathy with others and less confidence in our own self-sufficiency. We are humiliated and broken at His feet, poor and helpless. This is the best thing that can happen to us.

Temptation exercises our faith and teaches us to pray. It puts us under fire and compels us to exercise our weapons and prove their potency. It shows us the resources of Christ and the preciousness of the promises of God. It teaches us the reality of the Holy Spirit and compels us to walk closely with Him and hide continually behind His strength and all-sufficiency.

Every victory gives us new confidence in our victorious Leader and new courage for the next onset of the foe, so that we become not only victor, but more than conquerors, taking the strength of our defeated foes and gathering precious spoil from each new battlefield.

Wait on the Lord—Psalm 27:14.

*W*ait on the Lord. How often this is said in the Bible; how little understood! It is what the old monk called the "practice of the presence of God." It is the habit of prayer. It is the continual communion that not only asks, but receives. People often ask us to pray for them and we have to say, "Why, God has answered our prayer for you; now you must take the answer. It is awaiting you, and you must take it by waiting on the Lord."

It is this that renews our strength until we "mount up with wings as eagles, run and are not weary, walk and are not faint." Our hearts are too limited to take in His fullness at a single breath. We must live in the atmosphere of His presence till we absorb His very life. This is the secret of spiritual depth and rest, of power and fullness, of love and prayer, of hope and holy usefulness. *Wait, I say, on the Lord.*

> I am waiting in communion at the
>   blessed mercy seat;
> I am waiting, sweetly waiting on
>   the Lord;
> I am drinking of His fullness; I am
>   sitting at His feet;
> I am hearkening to the whispers
>   of His Word.

> *That good thing which was committed*
> *unto thee keep by the Holy Ghost*
> *—2 Timothy 1:14.*

God gives to us a power within which will hold our hearts in victory and purity. *That good thing which was committed unto thee keep by the Holy Ghost which dwelleth in us.* It is the Holy Spirit; and when any thought or suggestion of evil arises in our hearts, the quick conscience can instantly call upon the Holy Spirit to drive it out, and He will expel it at the command of faith or prayer and keep us as pure as we are willing to be kept. But when the will surrenders and consents to evil, the Holy Spirit will not expel it. God, then, requires us to stand in holy vigilance, and He will do exceeding abundantly for us as we hold fast that which is good. He will also be in us a spirit of vigilance, showing us the evil and enabling us to detect it and to bring it to Him for expulsion and destruction.

O Spirit of Jesus, fill us until we shall have room only for Thee.

> Oh, come as the heart-searching fire,
> Oh, come as the sin-cleansing flood;
> Consume us with holy desire,
> And fill with the fullness of God.

Now no chastening for the present seemeth to be joyous, but grievous: nevertheless afterward—Hebrews 12:11.

God seems to love to work by paradoxes and contradictions. In the transformations of grace, the bitter is the base of the sweet, night is the mother of day and death is the gate of life.

Many people want to have power. But, how is power produced? The other day I passed the large powerhouse where the trolley engines are supplied with electricity. I heard the hum and roar of countless wheels, and I asked my friend, "How do they make the power?" "Why," he said, "just by the revolution of those wheels and the magnetic friction they produce. The friction creates the electric current."

In this same manner, when God wants to bring more power into our lives, He brings more pressure. He is generating spiritual force by friction. Some of us do not like it. Some of us do not understand. We try to run away from the pressure instead of getting the power and using it to rise above the painful cause.

> O troubled soul, beneath the rod
> Thy Father speaks—be still, be still;
> Learn to be silent unto God,
> And let Him mold thee to His will.

They were all filled with the Holy Ghost
—Acts 2:4.

Blessed secret of spiritual purity, victory and joy, of physical life and healing and all power for service! Filled with the Spirit there is no room for self or sin, for fret or care. Filled with the Spirit we repel the elements of disease that are in the air as the red-hot iron repels the water that touches it. Filled with the Spirit we are always ready for service, and Satan turns away when he finds the Holy Spirit enrobing us in His garments of holy flame. Not half-filled, but *filled* with the Spirit—this is the place of victory and power!

It is not only a privilege; it is a command. And He who gave it will enable us to fulfill it if we bring it to Him with an empty, honest, trusting heart and claim our privilege in the name of Jesus and for the Glory of God.

> Holy Ghost, I bid Thee welcome;
> Come and be my Holy Guest;
> Heavenly Dove within my bosom,
> Make Thy home and build Thy nest;
> Lead me on to all Thy fullness,
> Bring me to Thy Promised Rest,
> Holy Ghost, I bid Thee welcome,
> Come and be my Holy Guest.

I have overcome the world—John 16:33.

Christ has overcome for us every one of our four terrible foes: Sin, Sickness, Sorrow, Satan. He has borne our sin, and we may lay all, even including our sinfulness itself, on Him. He has borne our sickness, and we may detach ourselves from our old infirmities and rise into His glorious life and strength. He has borne our sorrows, and we should not even carry a care, but rejoice evermore and even glory in tribulations. And He has conquered Satan for us, too, and left him nailed to the cross, spoiled and dishonored, a shadow of himself. And now we need only claim His full atonement and assert our victory, and so [*overcome*] *him by the blood of the Lamb and by the word of* [*our*]*testimony* (Revelation 12:11).

Beloved, are we overcoming sin? Are we overcoming sickness? Are we overcoming sorrow? Are we overcoming Satan?

> Fear not, though the strife be long;
> Faint not, though the foe be strong;
> Trust thy glorious Captain's power;
> Watch with Him one little hour,
> Hear Him calling, "Follow Me,
> I have overcome for thee."

> *Lean not unto thine own understanding*
> *—Proverbs 3:5.*

Faith is hindered by reliance upon human wisdom, whether our own or the wisdom of others. The devil's first bait to Eve was an offer of wisdom, and for this she sold her faith. *Ye shall be as gods,* he said, *knowing good and evil* (Genesis 3:5); and from that hour she began to know and she ceased to trust. It was the spies who postponed the Land of Promise to Israel. It was their "evil report" after searching out the land that led to the awful outbreak of unbelief and effectively shut the doors of Canaan to a whole generation. It is very significant that the names of those spies are nearly all suggestive of human wisdom, greatness and fame.

So in the days of Christ, it was the bondage of the Jews to the traditions of their fathers and the opinions of men that kept them back from receiving Him. *How can ye believe,* He asked, *which receive honour one of another; and seek not the honour that cometh from God only?* (John 5:44).

Let us trust Him with all our hearts and not lean upon our own understanding.

It is more blessed to give than to receive
—Acts 20:35.

How shall we know the difference between earthly and heavenly love? The one centers on ourselves and is partly our ego seeking its own gratification. The other reaches out to God and to people and finds its joy in glorifying Him and blessing them. Love is unselfishness, and the love that is not unselfish is not divine. How much do we give to others, and how much do we take for ourselves? What is the center of our being—ourselves, or our Lord and His people and work?

May the Lord help us to know more fully the meaning of that great truth, *It is more blessed to give than to receive. For whosoever will save his life shall lose it; but whosoever shall lose his life for my sake and the gospel's, the same shall save it* (Mark 8:35).

> Have you found some precious treasure?
> Pass it on.
> Have you found some holy pleasure?
> Pass it on.
> Giving out is twice possessing,
> Love will double every blessing,
> On to higher service pressing,
> Pass it on.

Pray ye therefore—Luke 10:2.

Prayer is the mighty force that will move missionary work. *Pray ye therefore the Lord of the harvest, that he will send forth labourers into his harvest* (Matthew 9:38).

We are asking God to touch the hearts of men every day by the Holy Spirit, so that they shall be compelled to go abroad and preach the gospel. We are asking Him to awaken them at night with the solemn conviction that the heathen are perishing and that their blood will be upon their souls. God is answering that prayer by sending persons to us every day who feel that *the king's business [requires] haste* (1 Samuel 21:8).

Beloved, pray, pray, pray. And as petitions rise to the heavens there will be a period of silence in heaven, and the coals of fire will be emptied out upon the earth, and the coming of the Lord will begin to draw nearer. Pray until the Lord of the harvest shall thrust forth laborers into His harvest.

> Send the coals of heavenly fire,
> From the altar of the skies;
> Fill our hearts with strong desire,
> Till our prayers like incense rise.

How ye ought to walk and to please God
—1 Thessalonians 4:1.

Many Christians are in the place that the Lord has appointed them, and yet the devil is harassing their lives with a sense that they are not quite pleasing the Lord. If they could just settle down in the place that God has assigned them and fill it faithfully and lovingly for Him, there would be more joy in their hearts and more power in their lives. God puts us in various places to serve Him, and the secret of accomplishing the most is to recognize our place as designated from Him and our service in it as pleasing to Him. Even in the great factory or the complex machine there is a place for the smallest screw and rivet as well as the great driving wheel and piston. So God has His "small parts" whose business is simply to stay where He puts them and to believe that He wants them there and is making the most of their lives in the little spaces that they fill for Him.

There is something all can do,
Tho' you're neither wise nor strong;
You can be a helper true,
You can stand when friends are few,
Some lone heart has need of you,
You can help along.

*The peace of God, which passeth all
understanding, shall keep your hearts
and minds—Philippians 4:7.*

It is not peace *with* God, but the peace *of* God
that [*keeps our*] *hearts and minds. The peace which
passeth all understanding* is the very breath of God in
the soul. He alone is able to keep it, and He can so
keep it that "nothing shall offend us." Is this your
experience?

God's rest did not come until His work was
finished. Nor will ours. We begin our Christian
lives by working, trying and struggling in the
energy of the flesh to save ourselves. At last,
when we are able to cease from our own work,
God comes in with His blessed rest and works
His own divine will in us.

> Oh! have you heard the glorious word
> Of hope and holy cheer?
> From heav'n above its tones of love
> Are lingering on my ear;
> The blessed Comforter has come,
> And Christ will soon be here.
>
> Oh hearts that sigh, there's succor nigh,
> The Comforter is near;
> He comes to bring us to our King,
> And fit us to appear.
> I'm glad the Comforter has come,
> And Christ will soon be here.

> *But ye are a chosen generation, . . . a peculiar people*—1 Peter 2:9.

Have you ever thought about the strange way in which God is calling a people out of a people already called? The word *ecclesia,* or church, means called out, but God is calling out a still more select body from the church to be His bride—those especially prepared for His coming.

We see an illustration of this in the story of Gideon. When first he sounded the trumpet of Abiezer there resorted to him more than thirty thousand men; however, he was instructed by God to reduce the number. A first test was applied, appealing to their courage, and all but ten thousand returned home. But there needed to be an additional elimination, and so a second test was applied appealing to their prudence, caution and singleness of purpose, and all but three hundred were refused.

With this small but select band, Gideon raised the standard against the Midianites. Through the power of God he won his glorious victory. So in this present day the Master is choosing His three hundred, and by them He will yet win the world for Himself. Let us be sure that we belong to the "out and out" people.

*They wandered in the wilderness in a
solitary way—Psalm 107:4.*

All who fight the Lord's battles must be content to die to the favorable opinions of men and the flattery of human praise. We cannot make an exception even in favor of the good opinions of the children of God. It is very easy for the insidious adversary to make this also an appeal to the flesh.

It is all right when God sends us the approval of our fellow men; however, we must never make that approval a motive in our life. All such motives are poison and deprive us of the strength with which we are to give glory to God. Rather, we must be content with the solitary way and the lonely wilderness.

The man of God must walk alone with God. He must be content in the realization that God knows all things. It is such a relief to the natural man within us to fall back upon human countenances and human thoughts and sympathy that we often deceive ourselves and think it "brotherly love," when, in fact, we are just resting in the earthly sympathy of some fellow worm!

Keep yourselves in the love of God
—Jude 21.

Some time ago, I was enjoying a beautiful sunset. The western skies seemed like a great archipelago of golden islands, the masses in the distance rising up into vast mountains of glory. The hue of the sky was so gorgeous that it seemed to reflect itself upon the whole atmosphere as I looked back from the west to the eastern horizon. The whole earth was radiant with glory. The fields had changed to strange red richness, and the earth seemed bathed with the dews of heaven.

So it is when the love of God shines through all our celestial sky; it covers everything below, and life becomes radiant with its light. Things that were hard become easy. Things that were biting become sweet. Labor loses its burden, and sorrow becomes silver-lined with hope and gladness.

There are two ways of living in God's love: one is constant trust; the other is constant obedience. God's own Word gives the message for both. *If ye keep my commandments, ye shall abide in my love; even as I have kept my Father's commandments, and abide in his love* (John 15:10).

···

We are his workmanship—Ephesians 2:10.

C hrist sends us to serve Him, not in our own strength, but in His resources and might. *For we are his workmanship, created in Christ Jesus unto good works, which God hath before [prepared] that we should walk in them* (Ephesians 2:10). We do not have to prepare them but to wear them as garments made to order for every occasion of our lives.

We must receive them by faith and go forth in His work, believing that He is with us and in us as our all-sufficiency for wisdom, faith, love, prayer, power and every grace and gift that our work requires. In this work of faith we shall have to feel weak and helpless and even have little consciousness of power. But if we believe and go forward, He will be the power and He will send the fruits.

The most useful services we render are those which, like the sweet fruits of the wilderness, spring from hours of barrenness. *[I] will bring her into the wilderness, . . . And I will give her her vineyards from thence* (Hosea 2:14-15). Let us learn to work as well as walk by faith. Then we shall receive the end of our faith, the salvation of precious souls, and our lives will bear fruit which shall be manifest throughout all eternity.

Continue ye in my love—John 15:9.

There are many different atmospheres in which one may live. Some people live in an atmosphere of thought. Their faces are thoughtful, their minds intellectual. They live in their ideas, their concepts of truth, their tastes and aesthetic nature. Other people live in their animal nature, in the lusts of the flesh and eye, the coarse, low atmosphere of a sensuous life, or worse. Still others live in a world of duty. The predominating feature of their lives is conscience, and it carries with it a certain shadowy fear that takes away the simple freedom and gladness of life. Admittedly, in the latter there is a rectitude, an uprightness, a strictness of purpose and of conduct which cannot be ignored or questioned.

But Christ bids us live in an atmosphere of love. *As my Father hath loved me, so have I loved you: continue ye in my love.* In the original it is, *live in my love.* Love is the atmosphere in which He would have us constantly live—that is, believing that He ever loves us and claiming His divine approval and tender regard. This is the life of love.

The Lord will give grace and glory
—Psalm 84:11.

This word *glory* is a very difficult one to translate, define or explain. But there is something in the spiritual consciousness of the quickened Christian that interprets it. It is the overflow of grace; it is the wine of life; it is the foretaste of heaven; it is a flash from the Throne and an inspiration from the heart of God which we may have and in which we may live. *The glory which thou gavest me I have given them* (John 17:22), the Master prayed for us. Let us take it and live in it. David used to say, *Wake up my glory*. Ask God to wake up your glory and enable you to mount up with wings as eagles, to dwell on high and sit with Christ in heavenly places.

> Mounting up with wings as eagles,
> Waiting on the Lord we rise,
> Strength exchanging, life renewing,
> How our spirit heavenward flies.
> Then our springing feet returning,
> Tread the pathway of the saint,
> We shall run and not be weary,
> We shall walk and never faint.

He hath remembered his covenant forever—Psalm 105:8.

As long as we struggle under law—that is, by our own effort—sin shall have dominion over us. But the moment we step from under the shadow of Sinai and throw ourselves upon the simple grace of Christ and His free and absolute gift of righteousness, the struggle is practically over. We take Him to be to us what He has pledged Himself to be—our righteousness of thought and feeling—and ask Him to keep us, in spite of everything that ever can be against us, in His perfect will and peace.

Do we really know and believe that this is the very promise of the gospel, the very essence of the new covenant? Do we believe Christ pledges Himself to put His law in our hearts, to cause us to walk in His statutes and to keep His judgments and do them? Do we know that this is the oath which He swore unto Abraham—*that he would grant unto us, that we being delivered out of the hand of our enemies might serve him without fear, in holiness and righteousness before him, all the days of our life?* (Luke 1:74-75). He has sworn to do this for us, and He is faithful that promised. Let us trust Him.

Neither shall any plague come nigh thy dwelling—Psalm 91:10.

W e know what it is to be fireproof or to be waterproof. But it is a greater thing to be sinproof. It is possible to be so filled with the Spirit of Jesus that all the shafts of the enemy glance off our heavenly armor. It is possible to so know the presence of Jesus that all the burrs and thistles which grow on the wayside fail to stick to our heavenly robes. All the noxious vapors of the pit disappear before the warm breath of the Holy Ghost, and we walk with a charmed life even through the valley of the shadow of death.

The red-hot iron repels the water that touches it and the fingers that would toy with it. If we have been set aflame by the Holy Spirit, Satan will keep his fingers off us, and the cold water that he pours over us will roll off and leave us unharmed. *We know that whosoever is born of God sinneth not; but he that is begotten of God keepeth himself, and that wicked one toucheth him not* (1 John 5:18).

Before going into a malarial region, it is well to fortify the system with nourishing food. So we should be fed and filled daily by the life of Christ in such a way that evil cannot invade our lives.

Launch out into the deep—Luke 5:4.

Many difficulties and perplexities in connection with our Christian lives might best be settled by a simple and bold decision of our will to go forward with the light we have, leaving the speculations and theories that we cannot decide for further settlement. What we need is to act, and to act with the best light we have. As we step out into the present duty and full obedience, many things will be made plain which it is no use waiting to decide.

Launch out into the deep with a bold plunge, and Christ will settle for you all the questions that you are now debating. More probably, He will show you their insignificance and let you see that the only way to settle them is to leap over them. They are Satan's petty snares to waste your time and keep you halting when you should be marching on.

> The mercy of God is an ocean divine,
> A boundless and fathomless flood;
> Launch out in the deep, cut away the
>   shoreline,
> And be lost in the fullness of God.

....

*They which receive abundance of grace and
of the gift of righteousness shall reign in
life—Romans 5:17.*

God's people sometimes fight tremendous
battles to attain to righteousness in trying
circumstances. Perhaps they feel guilt because
temptation has been allowed to overcome them
or, at least, to turn them aside from their singleness of purpose toward God. The resulting conflict is a terrible one as they seek to adjust and
be right with God. They find themselves baffled
by spiritual foes, and they are helpless and perplexed.

How dark and dreary the struggle! At such
times how helpless and ineffectual we seem to
be!

We are almost sure to strive in the spirit of the
law; such striving will always result in condemnation and failure. Every disobedience is
met by a blow of wrath and discouragement, and
we are close to despair.

If the tempted and struggling one could only
understand, or remember what perhaps he has
learned before, that Christ is our righteousness,
and that it is not by law but by grace alone that
we conquer. *For sin shall not have dominion over you:
for ye are not under the law, but under grace* (Romans
6:14). That is the secret of the battle.

Casting all your care upon him
—1 Peter 5:7.

There are some things that God will not tolerate in us. We must leave them. Nehemiah would not talk with Sanballat about his charges and fears. He simply refused to have anything to do with the matter—even to take refuge in the temple to pray about it.

How very few things we really have to do with in life. If we would only drop all the needless things and simply do the things that absolutely require our attention from morning till night, we would find what a small slender thread life is. But we string upon it a thousand imaginary beads and burden ourselves with cares and flurries that—if we had trusted more—would never have needed to preoccupy us.

Wise indeed was the testimony of the dear old saint who said, in review of her past life, "I have had a great many troubles in my life, especially those that never came."

> Trust and rest with heart abiding,
> Like a birdling in its nest,
> Underneath His feathers hiding,
> Fold thy wings and trust and rest.
> Trust and rest, trust and rest,
> God is working for the best.

*Hold fast the confidence and the rejoicing
of the hope firm unto the end
—Hebrews 3:6.*

The attitude of faith is simple trust. It is
Elijah saying to Ahab, *There is a sound of
abundance of rain* (1 Kings 18:41). But then there
comes usually a deeper experience in which the
prayer is inwrought. It is Elijah on the mount,
with his face between his knees, travailing, as it
were, in birth for the promised blessing. He has
believed for it and now he must take it. The first
is Joash shooting the arrow out of the window,
but the second is Joash smiting on the ground and
following up his faith by perseverance and victorious testing (2 Kings 13:14-25).

It is in this latter place that many of us fall
short. We ask much from God, and when God
proceeds to give it to us we are not found equal
to His expectation. *We are made partakers of Christ,
if we hold the beginning of our confidence steadfast unto
the end* (Hebrews 3:14), and trust Him through it
all.

> Fainting soldier of the Lord,
> Hear His sweet inspiring word,
> "I have conquered all thy foes.
> I have suffered all thy woes;
> Struggling soldier, trust in Me,
> I have overcome for thee."

He is a new creature
—2 Corinthians 5:17.

Resurrected, not raised. There is so much in this distinction. The teaching of human philosophy is that we are to raise humanity to a higher plane. But this is not the gospel. On the contrary, the teaching of the cross is that humanity must die and sink out of sight and then be resurrected, not raised.

Resurrection is not an improvement, not elevation; it is a new supernatural life lifting us from nothingness into God and making us partakers of the divine nature. It is a new creation. It is an infinite elevation above the highest plane. Let us refuse anything less than resurrection life.

> I am crucified with Jesus,
> And the cross has set me free;
> I have ris'n again with Jesus,
> And He lives and reigns in me.
>
> This the story of the Master,
> Through the cross He reached
>   the throne,
> And like Him our path to glory,
> Ever leads through death alone.

And again I say, Rejoice
—Philippians 4:4.

It is a good thing to rejoice in the Lord. Perhaps you found the first dose ineffectual. Keep on with your medicine, and when you cannot feel any joy, when there is no wellspring and no seeming comfort and encouragement, still rejoice, and count it all joy. Even when you fall into temptations, reckon the circumstance joy and delight, and God will make your reckoning good.

Do you suppose your Father will let you carry the banner of His victory and His gladness on to the front of the battle, and then cooly stand back and see you captured or beaten back by the enemy? Never! The Holy Spirit will sustain you in your bold advance and fill your heart with gladness and praise. You will experience an exhilaration and refreshing because of the fullness of His Spirit within.

Lord, teach me to rejoice in Thee, and to rejoice evermore.

> The joy of the Lord is the strength
> of His people,
> The sunshine that scatters their sadness
> and gloom;
> The fountain that bursts in the desert
> of sorrow,
> And sheds o'er the wilderness,
> gladness and bloom.

The beauty of holiness
—Psalm 29:2.

Someone remarked once that he did not know more disagreeable people than sanctified Christians. He probably meant people who only *professed* sanctification. There is an angular, hard, unlovely type of Christian character that has little relation to true holiness—at least, not the highest type of holiness. It is the skeleton without the flesh to cover it; it is the naked rock without the vines and foliage that cushion its rugged sides. Jesus was not only virtuous and pure, but He was also beautiful and full of the warm attractivenesss of love.

We read of different kinds of graces: *Whatsoever things are just, . . . whatsoever things are lovely, . . . [and] of good report* (Philippians 4:8). There are a thousand little graces in the Christian life that we cannot afford to ignore. In fact, the last stages in any work of art are always the finishing touches. So let us not wonder if God seems to spend a great deal of time in teaching us the little things that many might consider insignificant.

God would have His Bride without spot or even wrinkle.

Jesus the author and finisher of our faith
—Hebrews 12:2.

Add to your *faith,* do not add to yourself. This is where we make the mistake. We must not only enter the Christian life by faith, but we must advance by faith each step of the way. At every new stage we shall find ourselves as incompetent and unequal for the pressure as before, and we must take the grace and the victory simply by faith.

Is it courage you need? You must claim it by faith. Is it love? You must seek to possess His love, and He will give it. Is it faith itself? You must have the faith of God, and Christ in you will be the spirit of faith as well as the blessing that faith claims.

So your whole life, from beginning to end, is but Christ in you—in the exceeding riches of His grace. Thus your everlasting song will be: not I; *but Christ who liveth in me.*

> 'Tis so sweet to walk with Jesus,
> Step by step and day by day;
> Stepping in His very footprints,
> Walking with Him all the way.

··

What time I am afraid, I will trust in thee—Psalm 56:3.

I shall never forget a remark George Mueller once made in answer to a gentleman who asked him the best way to have strong faith. "The only way to learn strong faith," replied the patriarch of faith, "is to endure great trials. I have learned my faith by standing firm in severe testing." What Mr. Mueller said is very true. The time to trust is when all else fails. If we could only realize the value of our present opportunity. Even while we are passing through these great afflictions, we are being held in the very soul of the *strongest* faith. If we will only let go, He will teach us in these hours the mightiest hold upon this throne which we can ever know. *Be not afraid, only believe.* If you *are* afraid, just look up and say, *What time I am afraid, I will trust in thee,* and you will yet thank God for the school of sorrow which was to you the school of faith.

> O brother, give heed to the warning,
> And obey His voice today.
> The Spirit to thee is calling,
> Oh, do not grieve Him away.

The fruit of the Spirit is . . . goodness
—Galatians 5:22.

Goodness is a fruit of the Spirit. Goodness is just "Godness." It is being like God. And godlike goodness has special reference to the active benevolence of God. The apostle Paul gave us the difference between goodness and righteousness in Romans 5:7: *Scarcely for a righteous man will one die: yet peradventure for a good man some would even dare to die.* The righteous man is the man of stiff, inflexible uprightness, but he may be as hard as a granite mountainside. The good man is that mountainside covered with velvet moss and flowers and flowing with cascades and springs. Goodness respects "whatsoever things are lovely." It is kindness, affection, benevolence, sympathy, rejoicing with those who rejoice, and weeping with those who weep.

Lord, fill us with Thyself, and let us be God-persons and good persons and so represent Thy goodness.

> There are lonely hearts to cherish,
> While the days are going by;
> There are weary souls who perish,
> While the days are going by.

He will keep the feet of his saints
—1 Samuel 2:9.

Perils as well as privileges attend the higher Christian life. The nearer we come to God, the thicker the hosts of darkness in heavenly places. The safe place lies in obedience to God's Word, singleness of heart and holy vigilance.

When Christians speak of standing in a place where they do not need to watch, they are in great danger. Let us walk in intimate and holy confidence, yet with holy, humble watchfulness, and *He will keep the feet of his saints.*

Now unto him [who] is able to keep [us] from falling, and to present [us] faultless before the presence of his glory with exceeding joy, to the only wise God our Saviour, be glory and majesty, dominion and power, both now and forever. Amen (Jude 24-25).

What to do we often wonder,
As we seek some watchword true,
Lo, the answer God has given,
What would Jesus do?

When the shafts of fierce temptation,
With their fiery darts pursue,
This will be your heavenly armor,
What would Jesus do?

*I wish above all things that thou
mayest prosper and be in health, even
as thy soul prospereth—3 John 2.*

*I*n the way of righteousness is life; and in the pathway
thereof is no death (Proverbs 12:28). That is the
secret of healing. Be right with God. Live in the
consciousness of it and nothing can hurt you. All
the fiery darts of the devil will glance off the
breastplate of righteousness, and faith will be
stronger for every fierce assault. How true it is,
*Who is he that will harm you, if ye be followers of that
which is good?* (1 Peter 3:13). And how true also:
*Holding faith, and a good conscience; which some having
put away concerning faith have made shipwreck*
(1 Timothy 1:19).

And yet again: *If thou wilt diligently hearken to the
voice of the Lord thy God, and wilt . . . keep all his statutes, I will put none of these diseases upon thee which I
have brought upon the Egyptians: for I am the Lord that
healeth thee* (Exodus 15:26).

> There's a question God is asking
> Every conscience in His sight,
> Let it search thine inmost being,
> Is it right with God, all right?

What things soever ye desire, when ye
pray, believe that ye receive them, and ye
shall have them—Mark 11:24.

Faith is not working up by willpower a sort of
certainty that something is coming to pass.
Rather, it is seeing as an actual fact that God has
said this thing shall come to pass—and that it is
true—and then rejoicing to know that it is true.
It is simply resting and entering into it because
God has said it.

Faith turns the promise into a prophecy.
While it is merely a promise it is contingent upon
our cooperation. It may or may not be. But when
faith claims it, it becomes a prophecy and we go
forth feeling that it is something that must be
done because God cannot lie.

Faith is the answer from the throne saying, "It
is done." Faith is the echo of God's voice. Let us
catch it from on high. Let us repeat it and go out
to triumph in its glorious power.

> Hear the answer from the throne,
> Claim the promise, doubting one,
> God hath spoken, "It is done."
> Faith hath answered, "It is done";
> Prayer is over, praise begun,
> Hallelujah! It is done.

Vessels of mercy, which he had afore prepared unto glory—Romans 9:23.

Our Father is fitting us for eternity. A vessel fitted for the kitchen will find itself in the kitchen. A vessel for the art gallery or the reception room will generally find itself there at last.

What are we being fitted for? To be a garbage receptacle to hold all the trash that people pour into our ears? Or a vase to hold sweet fragrance and flowers for the King's palace? A harp of many strings to sound the melodies and harmonies of His love and praise? Each one of us is going to his own place. Let us be fitted now.

> The days of heaven are Christly days,
> The Light of heaven is He;
> So walking at His side, our day
> As the days of heaven would be.
>
> The days of heaven are endless days—
> Days of eternity;
> So may our lives and works endure
> While the days of heaven shall be.
>
> Walk with us, Lord, through all
>   the days,
> And let us walk with Thee;
> 'Till as Thy will is done in heaven,
> On earth so shall it be.

He shall dwell on high—Isaiah 33:16.

It is easier for a consecrated Christian to live a total life for God than to live a mixed life. A soul redeemed and sanctified by Christ is too large for the shoals and sands of a selfish, worldly, sinful life. The great motor vessel can sail in deep waters without an effort, but she can make no progress in the shallow pool. In the crowded harbor, the smallest tugboat is worth a dozen of her, but out in mid-ocean she can outdistance it in an hour.

Beloved, your life is too large, too glorious, too divine for the small place in which you are trying to live. Your purpose is too petty. Arise and dwell on high in the resurrection life of Jesus and in the inspiring hope of His blessed coming.

> Rise with thy risen Lord,
> Ascend with Christ above,
> And in the heavenlies walk with Him,
> Whom seeing not, you love.
>
> Walk as a heavenly race,
> Princes of royal blood;
> Walk as the children of the light,
> The sons and heirs of God.

My expectation is from him—Psalm 62:5.

W hen we believe for a blessing, we must take the attitude of faith and begin to act and pray as if we already had it. We must treat God as if He had given us our request. We must lean our weight upon Him for the thing that we have claimed and just take it for granted that He gives it and is going to continue to give it. This is the attitude of trust.

When a young woman is married, she at once falls into a new attitude and acts in accordance with the fact. So it is when we take Christ as our Savior, our Sanctifier, our Healer and our coming Lord. He expects us to fall into the attitude of recognizing Him in the very capacity that we have claimed. Therefore, expect Him to be to you all that you have trusted Him for.

> You may bring Him ev'ry care
>   and burden,
> You may tell Him ev'ry need in pray'r,
> You may trust Him for the darkest
>   moment
> He is caring, wherefore need you care?
>
> Faith can never reach its consummation,
> 'Til the victor's thankful song we raise:
> In the glorious city of salvation,
> God has told us all the gates are praise.

Resist the devil, and he will flee
—James 4:7.

Resist the devil, and he will flee from you.
This is God's promise and He will keep it.
If we resist the adversary, God will compel him
to flee and will give us the victory. Just as a citizen would claim the protection of his government against an outrage or injustice by violent
men, so we can at all times fearlessly defy and
resist Satan our enemy.

At the same time we are not to stand on the
adversary's ground by any attitude or disobedience. In so doing we give him a certain power
over us which, while God will restrain in great
mercy and kindness, He will not fully remove
until we get fully on holy ground. We must
therefore be armed with the breastplate of
righteousness as well as the shield of faith, if we
would successfully resist . . . *principalities, . . .*
powers, . . . rulers of the darkness of this world, . . .
[and] spiritual wickedness in high places (Ephesians
6:12).

> Your full redemption rights
> With holy boldness claim,
> And to the utmost fullness prove
> The power of Jesus' name.

*Many shall be purified, and made white,
and tried—Daniel 12:10.*

*M*any shall be purified, and made white, and tried.
This is the promise for the Lord's coming.
It is more than purity. It is to be made white, lus-
trous or bright. To be purified is to have sin
burned out; to be made white is to have the glory
of the Lord burned in. The one is cleansing; the
other is illumination and glorification. The Lord
has both for us, but in order for us to have both
we must be put into the fire to be tried. We must
be led into difficult and strange places where
Christ shall be more to us because of the very
extremity of the situation. We are approaching
these days. Indeed, they are already around us,
and they are the precursors of the Lord's coming.

*Blesssed is he that . . . keepeth his garments lest he
walk naked* (Revelation 16:15).

> There are voices in the air, filling men
> with hope and fear;
> There are signals everywhere that the
> end is drawing near;
> There are warnings to prepare, for the
> King will soon be here;
> Oh, it must be the coming of the Lord!

As we have many members in one body,
. . . so we, being many, are one body in
Christ—Romans 12:4-5.

Sometimes our communion with God is cut off or interrupted because of a grievance against a brother, or some lack of unity in the body of Christ. We try to come to the Lord, but we cannot because we are separated from some member of the Lord's body or because the freedom of His love is not flowing through every organic part.

It does not require a blow on the head to paralyze the brain. A blow upon some nerve may do it. A wound in some artery at the extremities may be fatal to the heart. Therefore we must stand in right relationship with all God's children. If we would keep our perfect communion with Christ Himself, we must meet in the body of Christ in honest, open fellowship.

Sometimes we will find that an altered attitude to one Christian will bring us into the flood tides of the Holy Spirit. It is impossible to have faith without love, or to have Christ alone without the fullness of fellowship with all His dear saints. *And whether one member suffer, all the members suffer with it; or one member be honoured, all the members rejoice with it* (1 Corinthians 12:26).

In him we live, and move
—Acts 17:28.

The hand of Gehazi, and even the staff of Elisha, could not heal the lifeless boy. It required the living touch of the prophet's own divinely quickened flesh to infuse vitality into the cold clay. Lip to lip, hand to hand, heart to heart, he must touch the child before life could thrill his pulseless veins.

We must come into personal contact with the risen Savior and have His very life quicken our mortal flesh before we can know the fullness and reality of His healing. This is the most frequent cause of failure. People are often trusting in something that has been done *to them,* or in something that *they have done,* or in something that *they have believed* intellectually. Their spirit, however, has not felt its way to the heart of Christ; they have not drawn His love into their being by the hunger and thirst of love and faith, and so they are not quickened. The greatest need of our souls and bodies is to know Jesus personally, to touch Him constantly, to abide in Him continually.

May we this day lay aside all things that could hinder our near approach to Him and walk hand in hand, heart to heart, with Jesus.

*A merry heart doeth good like a
medicine—Proverbs 17:22.*

King Solomon left among his wise sayings a
prescription for sick and sad hearts, and it
is one that we can safely take. *A merry heart doeth
good like a medicine.* Joy is the great restorer and
healer. Gladness of spirit will bring health to the
bones and vitality to the nerves when all other
tonics fail and all other sedatives cease to quiet.
Are you ill? Begin to rejoice in the Lord, and
your bones will flourish like an herb, and your
cheeks will glow with the bloom of health and
freshness. Worry, fear, distrust, care—all are
poisonous! Joy is balm and healing, and if you
will but rejoice, God will give power. He has
commanded you to be glad and rejoice, and He
never fails to sustain His children in keeping His
commandments. *Rejoice in the Lord always,* He
says. This means no matter how sad, how tempted, how sick, how suffering you are, rejoice in
the Lord just where you are—and begin this
moment.

> The joy of the Lord is the strength
>   of our body,
> The gladness of Jesus, the balm for
>   our pain,
> His life and His fullness, our fountain
>   of healing,
> His joy, our elixir for body and brain.

I do always those things that please him—John 8:29.

It is a good thing to keep short accounts with God. I was very much struck some years ago with an interpretation of the verse: *So then every one of us shall give account of himself to God* (Romans 14:12). The thought it conveys is that of accounting to God daily. For us judgment is passed as we lay down on our pillows each night.

This is surely the true way to live. It is the secret of great peace. It will be a delightful comfort when life is closing or at the Master's coming, to know that our account is settled and our judgment over. For us, then, there is only the waiting to hear the glad *Well done, good and faithful servant; . . . enter thou into the joy of thy Lord* (Matthew 25:21).

Step by step I'll walk with Jesus,
Just a moment at a time,
Heights I have not wings to soar to,
Step by step my feet can climb.

Jesus keep me closer—closer,
Step by step and day by day
Stepping in Thy very footprints,
Walking with Thee all the way.

Hold fast the confidence—Hebrews 3:6.

Seldom will we see a sadder wreck of even the highest, noblest Christian character than when the enemy has succeeded in undermining the simple trust of a child of God and lured him into self-accusation and condemnation. It is a fearful place when the believer allows Satan to take the throne and act as God, sitting in judgment on his every thought and act and keeping him in the darkness of ceaseless condemnation. Well indeed has the Apostle told us to hold firmly the shield of faith!

This is Satan's objective point in all his attacks upon us, to destroy our trust. If he can get us to lose our simple confidence in God, he knows that he will soon have us at his feet.

For the Christian who has known the sweetness of God's love to lose his perfect trust in God is enough to wreck both reason and life. Let us *hold fast the confidence and the rejoicing of [our] hope firm unto the end.*

> Fear not to take your place
> With Jesus on the throne,
> And bid the powers of earth and hell,
> His sovereign sceptre own.

··

Commit thy way unto the Lord
—Psalm 37:5.

Rarely have I heard a better definition of faith than one given by a dear old woman, as she answered the question of a young man on how to take the Lord for needed help. In her characteristic way, pointing her finger toward him, she said with great emphasis, "You've just got to believe that He's done it, and it's done."

The great danger with most of us is that after we ask God to do something, we do not believe it is done. Instead we keep on helping Him and getting others to help Him—superintending God.

Faith adds its *amen* to God's *yea,* and then takes its hands off, and lets God finish His work. Its language is, *Commit thy way unto the Lord; trust also in Him.* And God worketh.

> Lord, I give up the struggle,
> To Thee commit my way,
> I trust Thy Word forever,
> And settle it all today.

And when the people complained, it displeased the Lord—(They were as it were, complainers)—Numbers 11:1.

There is a very remarkable phrase in the book of Numbers, in the account of the murmuring of the children of Israel in the wilderness. It reads like this: "When the people, as it were, murmured." Like most marginal readings, it is better than the text, and a great world of suggestive truth lies back of that little sentence.

Many a vivid picture rises before our imagination of people who do not dare to sin openly and unequivocally but manage to do it "as it were" only. They do not lie overtly, but they evade, or equivocate or imply enough falsehood to escape a real conviction of conscience. They do not openly accuse God of unkindness or unfaithfulness, but they strike at Him through somebody else. They find fault with circumstances and people and things that God has permitted to come into their lives and, "as it were" murmur. Perhaps they do not go any farther than that. But they feel like doing so. If they dared they would "charge God foolishly."

These things were written for our warning.

....

Rejoice evermore—1 Thessalonians 5:16.

Whatever else you lose, do not lose your joy. Keep the spirit of spring. Rejoice evermore and again I say, rejoice.

The loss of Canaan began in the spirit of murmuring. *When the people murmured, they displeased the Lord.* The first break in their fellowship, the first falter in their advance, came when they began to doubt and grieve and fret.

Keep your heart from the perforations of depression, discouragement, distrust and gloom, for Satan cannot crush a rejoicing and praising soul.

Be on your guard against the beginning of sin. Don't let the first touch of evil be harbored. It is the first step that loses all. Let us keep so encased in the Holy Spirit and in the very life of Jesus that the evil cannot reach us!

The little fly on the inside of the windowpane may be attacked by the little bird on the outside, and it may seem to him that he is lost. But that thin pane of glass keeps him safely from all danger as certainly as if it were a mighty wall of iron.

I, if I be lifted up from the earth, will draw all men unto me—John 12:32.

A true and pure Christian life attracts the world. Men and women find no inducement whatever in the lives of mediocre Christians to interest them in practical religion, but they may be won at once by a true and victorious example. Men of the world tend to step directly into a life of entire consecration rather than into the intermediate state which is usually presented to them by the witnessing Christian.

There was a man, a very prominent citizen, who for half a century or more had lived without Christ. He was a man in public life, a man of irreproachable character and manners, a man of lofty intellect. Although he displayed a most winning spirit, he was utterly out of sympathy with the Christian life. At the close of a service for the promotion of deeper spiritual life, he stood to ask the prayers of the congregation, and before the end of the week he was himself a true and acknowledged follower of the Lord Jesus Christ. He had said, as he went home following the service, "If that is the religion of Jesus Christ, I want it."

Rooted and grounded in love
—Ephesians 3:17.

There is a very singular shrub which grows abundantly in the west and is to be found in all parts of Texas. The mesquite, sometimes called the "mosquito tree," is a very slim and willowy looking shrub and would seem to be of little use for any industrial purposes; but it has extraordinary roots growing like great timbers underground and possessing such qualities of endurance in all situations that it was once valued as pavement material. It is said that the city of San Antonio was once paved with these roots.

The mosquito tree reminds us of those Christians who make little show externally, but their growth is chiefly underground—out of sight in the depth of God. These are the men and women that God uses for the foundations of things, and for the pavements of that city of God which will stand when all earthly things have crumbled into ruin and dissolved into oblivion.

> Deeper, deeper let the living
>   waters flow;
> Blessed Holy Spirit! River of
>   Salvation!
> All Thy fullness let me know.

Quit you like men—1 Corinthians 16:13.

Be brave. Cowards always get hurt. Brave men generally come out unharmed. Jeremiah was a hero. He shrank from nothing. He faced his king and countrymen with dauntless bravery, and the result was he suffered no harm but came through the siege of Jerusalem without a hair being injured. Zedekiah, the cowardly king, was always afraid to obey God and be true, and the result was he at last met the most cruel punishment ever inflicted on a human being.

The men and women who from the beginning stand true to their convictions have the fewest tests. When God gives to you a hard trial, if you can stand the strain He may not repeat it. When Abraham offered up his son Isaac on Mount Moriah, it was a final testing for the rest of his life. Do not let Satan see that you are afraid of him, for he will pursue to the death if he thinks that he has a chance of getting you.

> Be true, be true,
> Whether friends be false or few,
> Whatsoe'er betide, ever at His side,
> Let Him always find you true.

He that ruleth his spirit [is better]
than he that taketh a city
—Proverbs 16:32.

Temperance is true self-government. It involves the grace of self-denial and the spirit of a sound mind. It is that poise of spirit that holds us quiet, self-possessed, composed, deliberate and subject to the voice of God and the conviction of duty in every step we take. Many persons do not have that poise and serenity. They are drifting at the impulse of their own impressions and moods, the influence of others or the circumstances around them.

No desire should ever control us. No purpose, however right, should have such mastery over us that we are not perfectly free. Our pure affection may be an inordinate affection. Our work itself may be a selfish passion. That thing that we began to do because it was God's will we may cling to and persist in, ultimately, because it is our own will.

Lord, give us a spirit ever controlled by Thy Spirit and will and the eye that looks to Thee every moment *as the eyes of a maiden to the hands of her mistress* (Psalm 123:2). So shall Thy service be our perfect freedom, and our subjection divinest liberty.

They shall mount up with wings
—Isaiah 40:31.

They shall mount up with wings as eagles is God's preliminary; the next promise is, *they shall run, and not be weary; and they shall walk, and not faint.* Hours of holy exultation are the reward for hours of patient plodding, waiting and working. Nature has its springs, and so has grace.

Let us rejoice in the Lord always. Let us take Him to be our continual joy, whose heart is a fountain of blessedness and who is anointed with the oil of gladness above His fellows.

We must not be disappointed if the tides are not always equally high. Even at low tide the ocean is just as full. Human nature could not stand perpetual excitement, even of a happy kind, and God often rests in His love.

Let us live as unselfconsciously as possible, filling up each moment with faithful service and trusting Him to stir the springs at His will. Then as we go on in faithful service, we shall hear, again and again, His glad whisper: *Well done, thou good and faithful servant: . . . enter thou into the joy of thy Lord* (Matthew 25:21).

Rest in the Lord, and wait patiently
for him—Psalm 37:7.

The Gospel of Mark, which is the gospel of service, contains a very suggestive thought. We hear the Master saying to His disciples, *Come ye apart into a desert place, and rest a while* (Mark 6:31). It is possible to possess an energy that may be tireless and ceaseless, and yet still as the ocean's depth. It is possible to know the peace of God which passes all understanding.

The two deepest secrets of rest are to be in harmony with the will of God and to trust. *Great peace have they that love thy law* (Psalm 119:165), expresses the first. *Thou wilt keep him in perfect peace, whose mind is stayed on thee: because he trusteth in thee* (Isaiah 26:3), describes the second.

There is much involved in learning to "stay." Sometimes we forget that it literally means to stop. It is a great blessing even to stop all thought. Often, the only way to counter the devil's whirlwind of irritating questions and thoughts is to be absolutely still, to refuse even to think and to meet his evil voice with a simple and everlasting No!

If we will be still, God will give us peace.

....

There they dwelt with the king for
his work—1 Chronicles 4:23.

It is easy for water to run down from the
upper springs, but it requires a divine impulse
for it to flow up from the valley in the subter-
ranean springs. There is nothing that tells more
of Christ than to see a Christian rejoicing and
cheerful in the humdrum and routine of commonplace work. He or she is like the sailors who
stand on the dock loading their vessel and singing
as they swing their loads. The praiseful Christian
is keeping time in spirit with the footsteps and
movements of labor and duty.

No one has a sweeter or higher ministry for
Christ than men and women at their regular
occupations who can carry the light of heaven in
their faces all day long. Certain sea fowl can
plunge beneath the ocean's surface and come
forth without one drop of water adhering to
their beautiful plumage, burnished breasts and
glowing wings. On their feathers is a subtle oil
that keeps the water from sticking. So, thank
God, we too may be anointed with the Holy
Spirit to the extent that sin, sorrow and defilement will not adhere to us. Instead, we shall pass
through every sea as the ship passes through the
waves—in, but above the floods around us.

The anointing which ye have received
—1 John 2:27.

Divine anointing is the secret of the deeper life, but *that ye [may be] rooted and grounded in love* (Ephesians 3:17) is the substance and sweetness of it.

The fullness of the divine love in the heart will make everything easy. It is very easy to trust those whom we love, and the more we realize their love the more we will trust them for it. This love is the source of healing. The tide of love flowing through our bodies will strangely strengthen our very frame and the spring of youth and freshness in our physical being.

The secret of love is very simple. It is to take the heart of Jesus for our love and claim His love for every need of life, whether it be toward God or toward others. It is very satisfying to think of other persons in this way. "I will take the heart of Jesus toward them, to let me love them as He loves them." Then we can love even the unworthy in some measure, if we see them in the light of His love—as they shall be and not as they now are, unworthy of our love.

··

Christis the head—Ephesians 5:23.

Often we want people to pray for us and help us, but we always defeat our object when we look too much to them and lean upon them. The true secret of union is for both to look upon God, and in the act of looking past themselves to Him they are unconsciously united.

The sailor was right when he saw the little boy fall overboard and waited a minute before he plunged to his rescue. When the distracted mother asked him in agony why he had waited so long, he calmly replied: "I knew that if I went in sooner he would clutch at me and drag me down. I waited until his struggles were over, and then I was able to help him when he did not grasp me too tightly."

When people grasp us too strongly, either with their love or with their dependence, we are intuitively conscious that they are not looking to God, and we become paralyzed in our efforts to help them. United prayer, therefore, requires that the one for whom we pray be looking away from us to the Lord Jesus Christ, and we *together* look to Him alone.

*For we have not an high priest which
cannot be touched with the feeling of our
infirmities—Hebrews 4:15.*

S ome time ago I was talking with a greatly
suffering woman about healing. She was
quite burdened physically and sincerely wanted
to be able to trust the Lord for deliverance.
After a short conversation I prayed with her,
committing her case to the Lord, asking that in
absolute trust she might claim deliverance.

As soon as I ended my prayer she grasped my
hand and asked me to unite with her in the burden that was most upon her heart. And then,
without a word of reference to her own healing
or the burden under which she was being crushed
to death, she burst into an impassioned prayer for
an orphan boy of whom she had just heard that
day. Never have I heard a prayer surpass it for
sympathy and love, as she implored God in ago-
nizing sobs to help him and save him. And then
she ceased without even referring to her own
need.

I was deeply touched by the spectacle of love,
and I thought how the Father's heart must be
touched for her own need.

....

Fret not thyself in any wise
—Psalm 37:8.

A life was lost in Israel because a pair of human hands were laid unbidden upon the ark of God. They were placed upon it with the best intent to steady the ark as the oxen drew the cart carrying it along the rough way. But they touched God's work presumptuously, and they fell paralyzed and lifeless.

Much of the life of faith consists in letting things alone. If we wholly trust an interest to God we can keep our hands off it, and He will guard it for us better than we can help Him. *Rest in the Lord, and wait patiently for him: fret not thyself because of him who prospereth in his way, because of the man who bringeth wicked devices to pass* (Psalm 37:7).

Things may seem to be going all wrong, but He knows better than we, and He will arise in the right moment if we are really trusting Him completely enough to let Him work in His own way and time. There is nothing so effective as inactivity in some things, and there is nothing so damaging as restless working, for God has undertaken to work His sovereign will.

··

The very God of peace sanctify you
wholly—1 Thessalonians 5:23.

The great tide is bearing up the stranded ship until she floats above the sand bar with neither straining seam nor struggling seaman. No need now for the ineffectual and toilsome efforts of the crew and the strain of the engines which had tried in vain to move her an inch before that heavenly impulse lifted her by its own attraction.

God lifts up, by means of His sunbeams, the mighty iceberg which a million men could not raise a single inch, but which melts away before the sun's warm rays and rises in vapor clouds to meet its embrace until that cold and heavy mass is floating in glorious fleecy clouds in the blue ocean of the sky.

How easy all this! How mighty! How simple! How divine! Beloved, have you come into the divine life of holiness? If you have, how your heart must swell with gratitude! If you have not, do you not long for it, and will you not unite in the prayer of the text that the very God of peace will sanctify you wholly?

Strangers and pilgrims—Hebrews 11:13.

If you have ever tried to plough a straight furrow in the country—I feel sorry for the man who does not know how to plough and more sorry for the man who is too proud to want to know—you have no doubt found it necessary to have two stakes in a line and to drive your horses by these stakes. If you have only one stake before you, you will have no steadying point for your vision, and you can swerve about without knowing it, making your furrows as crooked as a serpent's coil. But if you have two stakes and always keep them in line, you cannot deviate an inch from a straight line, and your furrow will be as an arrow speeding to its target.

This can be a great lesson to us in our Christian lives. If we would run a straight course, we must have two stakes—the near and the distant. It is not enough to be living in the present; it is likewise a great and glorious thing to have a distant goal.

The sweetness of the lips
—Proverbs 16:21.

Spiritual conditions are inseparably connected with our physical life. The flow of the divine life-currents may be interrupted by a little clot of blood; the vital current may leak out through a very small wound.

If you want to keep the health of Christ, keep from all spiritual infections, from all heart wounds and irritations. One hour of worry will wear out more vitality than a week of work; one minute of malice or jealousy or envy will hurt more than a drink of poison. Pleasantness of spirit and joyousness of heart are essential to full health. Quietness of spirit, gentleness, tranquility and the peace of God that passes all understanding are worth more than all the sleeping pills in the country.

We do not wonder that some people have poor health when we hear them talk for half an hour. They have enough dislikes, prejudices, doubts and fears to exhaust the strongest constitution.

My friend, if you would maintain God's life and strength, keep out the things that kill it. Keep yourself for Him and for His work, and you will find enough and to spare.

For it is God which worketh in you
—Philippians 2:13.

S anctification is the gift of the Holy Spirit, the fruit of the Spirit, the grace of the Lord Jesus Christ and the prepared inheritance of all who enter in. It is the obtainment of faith, not the attainment of works. It is divine holiness, not human self-improvement or perfection. It is the inflow into man's being of the life and purity of the infinite, eternal and Holy One. It is the bringing in of God's own perfection and the working out of His own will.

How easy, how spontaneous, how delightful this heavenly way of holiness! Surely it is a "highway" and not the low way of man's vain and fruitless mortification. It is God's great elevated railway, sweeping over the heads of the struggling throngs who toil along the lower road when they might be borne along on His ascension pathway by His own almighty impulse. It is God's great elevator carrying us up to the higher chambers of His palace, without arduous efforts, while others struggle up the winding stairs and faint by the way.

Let us today so fully take Him that He can *cause [us]* to walk in *[his] statutes* (Ezekiel 36:27).

That I might finish my course with joy—Acts 20:24.

This is a most serious thought, this thought of finishing our work. There is nothing in the Christian life quite so sad as unfinished work.

As I look over the work of God, I see strewn all along the way this curse of incompleted work. The book of Judges tells us of five hundred years of declension because God's people did not complete their work when they were in possession of Canaan. They conquered Jericho; they conquered 31 kingdoms; they divided the land among 12 victorious tribes; but they left here and there little strongholds that were not subdued—little tribes that could not or would not be driven out—and it was not long until they brought Israel under subjection and neutralized all the work of Joshua's conquest.

Consider the ministry of Elijah. Never has the world seen anything more sublime than his victory on Carmel. But who has not grieved at his reaction on the following day when, at the shaking of a woman's finger, he fled into the desert and left the field in possession of God's enemies.

It is not enough to go on for a while. It is the last step that wins. May God put on our hearts this thought, *that I might finish my course with joy, and the ministry, which I have received of the Lord Jesus, to testify the gospel of the grace of God.*

Love believeth all things
—1 Corinthians 13:7.

There is a beautiful expression in the book of Isaiah which reflects with accuracy the depth of the love of God. He said, *They are my people, children that will not lie: so he was their Saviour* (Isaiah 63:8). They lied, but He would not believe it. At least He speaks as if He would not believe it, in the greatness of His love, because they were His people. He has not seen iniquity in Jacob nor perversity in Israel. There is plenty of it to see, and the devil sees it all, and a good many people are only too glad to see it, but the dear Father will not see it. He covers it with His love and the precious blood of His atoning Son.

Such a wonderful love ought surely to make us more gentle to others and more anxious to cause our Father less need to hide His loving eyes from our imperfections and faults.

If we have the mind and heart of Christ, we shall clothe even the non-Christians with those graces which faith can claim for them. We shall try our best to count them as if they were real, and by love and prayer we shall at length make them real. *Love believeth all things* (1 Corinthians 13:7).

The fruit of the Spirit is . . .
gentleness—Galatians 5:22.

Nature's harshness has melted away and she is now beaming with the smile of spring, and everything around us whispers of the gentleness of God. This beautiful fruit is in lovely harmony with the gentle month of which it is the keynote. May the Holy Spirit lead us these days into His purity, quietness and gentleness, subduing every coarse, rude, harsh and unholy habit. May He make us like Him—of whom it is said, *He shall not strive, nor cry; neither shall any man hear his voice in the streets* (Matthew 12:19).

The man who is truly filled with Jesus will always be a gentleman. The woman who is baptized of the Holy Spirit will have the instincts of a perfect lady, although lowborn and untutored in the schools of earthly refinement. Let us receive and reflect the gentleness of Christ until the world will say of us, as the polished infidel Chesterfield once said of the saintly Fenelon, "If I had remained in his house another day, I should have had to become a Christian."

Lord, help us today to so yield to the gentle Dove-Spirit that our lives shall be as His life.

Always causeth us to triumph
—2 Corinthians 2:14.

How these words help us! Think of them when people rasp you, when the devil pricks you with his fiery darts, when your sensitive, self-willed spirit chafes or frets. Let a gentle voice be heard above the strife, whispering, "Keep sweet, keep sweet!" And, if you will but heed it quickly, you will be saved from a thousand falls and kept in perfect peace.

True, we cannot keep ourselves sweet, but God will keep us if He sees that it is our fixed, determined purpose to be kept sweet, and to refuse to fret or bear a grudge or retaliate. The trouble is, we may at times enjoy a little irritation and morbidness. We want to cherish the little grudge, and sympathize with our hurt feelings and nurse our little grievance.

God will give us all the love we really want and honestly choose. We can have our grievance, or we can have the peace that passeth all understanding; but we cannot have both.

There is a balm for a thousand heartaches, and a heaven of peace and power in these two little words—*keep sweet.*

···

My peace I give unto you—John 14:27.

Here lies the secret of abiding peace—God's peace. We give ourselves to God and the Holy Spirit takes possession of our hearts. It is indeed "Peace, peace." But it is at this precise point that the devil begins to interfere, and he does it through our thoughts, diverting or distracting them as the occasion requires.

This is the time to prove the sincerity of our consecration and the singleness of our hearts. If we truly desire His presence more than anything, we will turn away from every conflicting thought and look steadily up to Jesus. But if we desire the gratification of our impulses more than His presence, we will yield to the passionate word, or the frivolous thought, or the sinful diversion. Then when we come back, our Shepherd has gone, and we wonder why our peace has departed.

Failure occurs often in some insignificant thing—usually a thought or word. The soul that would not fear to climb a mountain may actually stumble over a straw.

The real secret of perfect rest is to be jealously, habitually occupied with Jesus.

···

*Greater is he that is in you, than he
that is in the world—1 John 4:4.*

S atan loves to trip us over little things. The
reason for this is that it is generally a greater
victory for him and shows that he can upset us by
a shaving and knock us down with a straw. It is
the old boast of the Jebusites, when they told
David they could defend Jerusalem by a garrison
of the blind and lame.

Most of us manage better in our great struggles than we do in our minor ones. It was over a
little piece of fruit that Adam fell, but all the
world was wrecked. Keep a close watch for the
little stumbling blocks and do not let Satan laugh
at you and tell his demons how he tripped you
over a banana peel. Then, too, when the devil
wants to hinder some great blessing in our lives,
he generally throws some ugly shadow over it
and makes it look distasteful to us. How many
times has the devil succeeded in preventing us
from receiving God's greatest blessing by keeping us from certain truths or places or persons
which we avoided because of our false or foolish
prejudice!

If ye then be risen—Colossians 3:1.

God is waiting today to mark the opening hours, for every ready and willing heart, with a touch of life and power that will lift us to higher pleasures and offer to our vision grander horizons of hope and holy service.

We shall not need to look far to discover our risen Lord. He was in advance even of the earliest seeker that Easter morning, and He will be waiting for us before the break of day with His glad "All hail" if we only have eyes to see and hearts to welcome and obey Him.

What is His message to us this springtime? *If ye then be risen with Christ, seek those things which are above, where Christ sitteth on the right hand of God. For ye are dead, and your life is hid with Christ in God* (Colossians 3:1, 3).

It is not just *risen* with Christ, but *resurrected*. It is not rising a little higher in the old life, but it is rising from the dead. The resurrection will mean no more than the death has meant. Only so far as we are really dead shall we live with Him.

Reckon ye also yourselves to be . . . alive unto God—Romans 6:11.

D eath is but for a moment; life is forever. Let us live, then, as children of the resurrection, finding His glorious life more and more abundant, and the fullness of this life will repel the intrusion of self and sin and overcome evil with good. Then our existence will not be the dreary repression of our own struggling, but the springing tide of Christ's spontaneous overcoming life.

Once in a religious meeting a dear pastor gave us a most exhilarating talk on the risen life. Then another minister got up and talked for a long time on the necessity of self-crucifixion. A cold feeling came over us all and we could scarcely understand why. But after he had finished, one of the women clarified the whole situation by saying, "Pastor S. took us all out of the grave, and then Pastor P. put us back again."

Let us not go back into the grave once we have been delivered, but let us live like Christ, who *liveth and was dead; and, behold, [he is] alive forevermore, and [has] the keys of hell and of death* (Revelation 1:18). Let us keep out of the tomb. Keep the door locked and the keys in Christ's risen hands!

··

I travail in birth again until Christ
be formed in you—Galatians 4:19.

I t is a blessed moment when we are born again
and a new heart is created in us after the
image of God. It is a more blessed moment when,
in this new heart, Christ Himself is born and
Christmas time is reproduced in us as we, in some
real sense, become incarnations of the living
Christ. This is the deepest and holiest meaning of
Christianity. It is expressed in Paul's prayer for
the Galatians. *My little children, of whom I travail in*
birth again until Christ be formed in you.

There will yet be a more glorious era when
we, like Him, shall be transformed and transfigured into His glory, and in the resurrection shall
be, in spirit, soul and body, even as He.

Let us be, under the power of the inspiring
thought, incarnations of Christ, not living our
life, but the Christ life, and showing forth the
excellencies, not of ourselves, but of Him who
hath called us *out of darkness into his marvelous light.*
As a result our lives shall be to all the reliving of
the Christ life, as He would have lived it had He
been here.

Except a corn of wheat fall into the ground and die—John 12:24.

Death and resurrection are the central ideas of nature and Christianity. We see them in the transformation of the chrysalis, in the buried seed bursting into the bud and blossom of spring, in the transformation of the cold shroud of winter into the tinted robes of spring. We see it throughout the Bible in the symbol of circumcision with its significance of death and life, in the crossing of the Red Sea and the Jordan leading out and leading in, and in the cross of Calvary and the open grave of the Easter morning.

We see it in every deep spiritual life. Every true life is death-born, and the deeper the dying the truer the living. No doubt the passing months have shown us all many places where there ought to be a grave, and many lingering remnants of the natural and sinful which we ought gladly to commit to a bottomless grave. God help us to pass upon them the irrevocable sentence of death and to let the Holy Spirit make the interment eternal. Then our life shall be continually budding and blossoming and shedding fragrance over all.

All hail—Matthew 28:9.

It was a stirring greeting which the Lord of Life spoke to His first disciples on the morning of the resurrection. It is a bright and radiant word which, in His Name, we would speak to His beloved children at the commencement of another day.

It means a good deal more than appears on the surface. It is really a prayer for our health, but which none but those who believe in the healing of the body can fully understand. A thoughtful friend suggested once that the word "hail" really means health, and it is just the old Saxon form of the word. We all know that a hale person is a healthy person. Our Lord's message, therefore, was substantially that greeting which from time immemorial we give to one another when we meet: "How is your health?" "How are you?" or, better still, "I wish you health."

Christ's wish is equal to a promise and command. It is very similar to the apostle John's benediction to his dear friend Gaius, and we would re-echo it to our beloved friends according to the fullness of the Master's will. *I wish above all things that thou mayest prosper and be in health, even as thy soul prospereth* (3 John 2).

....

I am alive forevermore
—Revelation 1:18.

H ere is the message of the Christ of the cross and the still more glorious and precious Christ of the resurrection. It is beautiful and inspiring to note the touch of light and glory with which these simple words invest the cross. It does not say, *I am he that was dead and liveth,* but *I am he that liveth and was dead; and, behold, I am alive forevermore.* Life is mentioned before the death.

There are two ways of looking at the cross. One is from the death side and the other from the life side. One is the *Ecce Homo* (behold the man) and the other is the glorified Jesus with only the marks of the nails and the spear. It is thus we are to look at the cross. We are not to carry about with us the mold of the sepulcher, but the glory of the resurrection. It is not the *Ecce Homo,* but the Living Christ.

Our crucifixion is to be so complete that it shall be lost in our resurrection, and we shall even forget our sorrow and carry with us the light and glory of the eternal morning. So let us live the death-born life, ever new and full of a life that can never die because it is *dead and alive forevermore.*

....

*Whosoever will save his life shall
lose it—Luke 9:24.*

First and foremost Christ teaches resurrection and life. The power of Christianity is life. It brings us not merely law, duty, example, with high and holy teaching and admonition; it brings us the power to follow the higher ideal and the life that spontaneously does the things commanded. And it is not only life, but resurrection life.

It begins with a real crisis, a definite transaction, a point of time as clear as the morning dawn. It is not an everlasting dying and an eternal struggle to live. But it is all expressed in a tense that denotes definiteness, fixedness and finality. We actually died at a certain point and as actually began to live the resurrection life.

Let us reckon ourselves to be *dead indeed unto sin, but alive unto God through Jesus Christ* (Romans 6:11).

> And death is only the pathway
>   and portal
> To the life that shall die nevermore;
> And the cross leadeth up to the crown
>   everlasting,
> The Jordan to Canaan's bright shore.

*Tell me . . . where thou makest thy flock
to rest at noon—Song of Solomon 1:7.*

Beloved, do you not long for God's quiet,
the inner chambers, the shadow of the Almighty, the secret of His presence? Your life has
been, perhaps, all driving and doing; or perhaps
straining, struggling, longing and not obtaining.
You long for rest! You long to lie down close to
His heart and know that you have all in Him, that
every question is answered, every doubt settled,
every interest safe, every prayer answered,
every desire satisfied. Lift up the cry, *Tell me, O
thou whom my soul loveth, where thou feedest, where
thou makest thy flock to rest at noon!*

Blessed be His name! He has for us His exclu-
sive love—a love which each individual feels is
all for himself, one in which he can lie alone upon
His breast and have a place which no other can
dispute. And yet His heart is so great that He can
hold a thousand millions just as near, and each
heart seems to possess Him as exclusively for his
own as the thousand little pools of water upon
the beach can reflect the sun, and each little pool
appears to have the whole sun captured in its
beautiful depths. Christ can teach us this secret
of His inmost love.

Abide in me—John 15:4.

Christianity may mean nothing more than a religious system. The Christian life may mean nothing more than an earnest and honest attempt to follow and imitate Christ.

The Christ life is more than these and expresses our actual union with the Lord Jesus Christ. He is actually in us as the life and source of all our experience and work.

This conception of the highest Christian life is at once simpler and more sublime than any other. We do not teach that the purpose of Christ's redemption is to restore us to Adamic perfection, for if we had it we should lose it tomorrow. Rather, it is to unite us with the second Adam, and to lift us up to a higher plane than our first parents ever knew.

This is the only thing that can reconcile the warring elements of diverse schools of teaching with respect to Christian life. The Spirit of God will lead us to have no controversy respecting mere theories. Rather, we are simply to hold to the person and life of Jesus Christ Himself and the privilege of being united to Him through living in constant dependence upon His keeping power and grace.

But God—Luke 12:20.

Whenhat else do we really need? What else is He trying to make us understand? The religion of the Bible is wholly supernatural. The one resource of faith has always been the living God, and Him alone. The children of Israel were utterly dependent upon Jehovah as they marched through the wilderness. The one reason their foes feared them and hastened to submit themselves was that they recognized among them the shout of a King and the presence of One compared with whom all their strength was vain.

Wherein, asked Moses, *shall it be known here that I and thy people have found grace in thy sight? Is it not in that thou goest with us?* (Exodus 33:16). A church relying on human wisdom, wealth or resources ceases to be the body of Christ and becomes an earthly society. When we dare to depend entirely upon God and do not doubt, the humblest and feeblest agencies will become *mighty through God, to the pulling down of strongholds* (2 Corinthians 10:4).

May the Holy Spirit give to us at all times His own conception of these two great words, *But God!*

....

I press toward the mark
—Philippians 3:14.

We have thought much about what we have received. Let us think of the things we have not received, of some of the vessels that have not yet been filled, of some of the places in our lives that the Holy Spirit has not yet possessed for God and signalized by His glory and His presence.

Shall the coming months be marked by a diligent, heart-searching application of *the rest of the oil* (see Leviticus 14:17-20) to the yet unoccupied possibilities of our life and service?

Have we known His fullness of grace in our spiritual lives? Have we tasted a little of His glory? Have we believed His promise for the mind, the soul, the spirit? Have we known all His possibilities for the body? Have we tested Him in His power to control the events of nature and to move the hearts of men and nations? Has He opened to us the treasure house of God and met our financial needs as He might? Have we begun to understand the ministry of prayer, as God would have us exercise it? God give us *the rest of the oil!*

*It is not in man that walketh to direct
his steps—Jeremiah 10:23.*

United to Jesus Christ as our Redeemer, we
are accepted in the Beloved. He does not
merely take our place as a man and settle our
debts. He does that and more. He comes to give a
perfect ideal of what a man should be. He is the
model man, not for us to copy, for that would
only bring discouragement and utter failure; but
He will come and reproduce Himself in us.

If Christ lives in me, I am another Christ. I am
not like Him, but I have the same mind. The very
Christ is in me. This is the foundation of Christian holiness and divine healing. Christ is developing a perfect life within us. Some say man can
never be perfect. *It is not in man that walketh to
direct his steps.* We are all failures. This is true, but
we should go further. We must take God's provision for our failure and rise above it through His
grace. We must take Jesus as a substitute for our
miserable selves. We must give up the good as
well as the bad and take Him instead. It is hard
for us to learn that we must relinquish even the
good in order that we will depend upon divine
impulses rather than even our best attainments.

To him that overcometh, will I give
—Revelation 2:17.

A precious secret of Christian life is to have Jesus dwelling within the heart and conquering things that we never could overcome. It is the only secret of power in our lives. Men cannot understand it nor will the world believe it, but it is true that God will come to dwell within us and be the power, the purity, the victory and the joy of our lives. Our attitudes will no longer be, "What is the best that I can do?" but we will ask, "What is the best that Christ can do?" It enables us to say with Paul in that beautiful passage in Philippians, *I know both how to be abased, and I know how to abound: every where and in all things I am instructed both to be full and to be hungry, both to abound and to suffer need. I can do all things through Christ which strengtheneth me* (4:12-13).

With this knowledge I go forth to meet my testings, and this knowledge enables me to stand. I could never keep myself, but because Christ has met the adversary and defeated him for me I am kept pure and clean. *Thanks be to God, which giveth us the victory through our Lord Jesus Christ* (1 Corinthians 15:57).

For ye are dead—Colossians 3:3.

This definite, absolute and final putting off of ourselves in an act of death is something we cannot do ourselves. It is not self-mortifying, but it is dying *with* Christ. Nothing can do it but the cross of Christ and the Spirit of God.

The church is full of half-dead people who have been trying to slay themselves for years and have not had the courage to strike the fatal blow. Yet if they would just put themselves at Jesus' feet and let Him do it, there would be accomplishment and rest. On the cross He provided for our death as well as our life, and our part is just to let His death be applied to our nature as it has been to our old sins. When we have done this we must leave it all with Him, think no more about it and count it dead. Recognizing it as no longer ourselves, but another, we must refuse to obey it, or fear it, to be identified with it, or even try to cleanse it. We must consider it utterly in His hands—and dead to us forever—and depend on Him for every breath of our new life as a new-born baby depends upon the life of its mother.

*He purgeth it, that it may bring forth
more fruit—John 15:2.*

Recently I passed a garden. The gardener had finished his pruning and the wounds of the knife and saw were just beginning to heal. The warm April sun was gently nourishing the stricken plant into fresh life and energy.

As I looked at that plant I thought how cruel it would be were the owner to begin next week to cut it down. The gardener's business now is to revive and nourish it into life. Its business is not to die, but to live.

So it is with the discipline of the soul. It, too, has its dying hour, but it must not always be dying. Rather we are to reckon ourselves to be dead unto sin, but alive unto God through Jesus Christ our Lord.

Death is but a moment. We should live, then, as children of the resurrection, depending more and more on His glorious life. The fullness of our lives will then repel the intrusion of self and sin and overcome evil with good. Our existence will not then be the dreary repression of our own struggling but the springing tide of Christ's spontaneous overcoming and everlasting life.

Ye are not your own
—1 Corinthians 6:19.

What a privilege that we may consecrate ourselves! What a mercy that God will take such worthless creatures! What rest and comfort lie hidden in those words, "Not your own." We are not responsible for our salvation, not burdened by our cares, not obliged to live for our interests, but altogether His. We are redeemed, owned, saved and kept in the strong, unchanging arms of His everlasting love.

What unbroken rest from sin and self and destructive care which true consecration brings! To be able to give Him our poor weak lives, with their awful possibilities and their utter helplessness, and know that He will accept them and take joy and pride in making out of them the utmost possibilities of blessing, power and usefulness. To give all, and find in so doing we have gained all! To be so yielded to Him in entire self-surrender that He is bound to care for us as for Himself! In such a step of consecration we are putting ourselves in the hands of a loving Father, more solicitous for our good than we can be and only wanting us to be fully submitted to Him that He may be freer to bless us.

*We will come unto him, and make our
abode with him—John 14:23.*

The Bible has always held out two great
promises respecting Christ. First, He will
come to us. Second, He will come into us.

For four thousand years the world looked forward to the fulfillment of the first promise. The
other is the secret which Paul says *hath been hid
from ages and from generations, but now is made manifest
to his saints, which is Christ in you the hope of glory*
(Colossians 1:26-27). This is just as great a revelation of God as the incarnation of Jesus, for it
makes us like Christ, as free from sin as He is.

If Christ is in us, what will be the conse-
quences? Why, He will put us aside entirely. The
I in us will go. We will say, "Not I, but
Christ." Christ undertakes our battles for us.
Christ becomes purity and grace and strength in
us.

We do not try to attain these things; we have
obtained them in Jesus. This brings glorious rest
with the Master. Jesus does not say, "Now we
must bring forth fruit, we must pray much, we
must do this or that." There is no constraint
about it, except that we must abide in Him. That
is the center of all joy and help.

···

Fight the good fight of faith
—1 Timothy 6:12.

How must God feel when we disappoint Him after He has given us His heart's blood, put so many advantages in our way and expended upon us so much grace and care. It makes the spirit cry, "Who is sufficient for these things?"

In my mind's eye I can see before me the time when we shall stand on heaven's shore and look back upon the years that have been, these few short years of time. May we cast ourselves at Jesus' feet and say: "Many a time have I faltered; many a hard fight has come, but Thou hast kept me and held me, thanks to God, who has given me the victory through the Lord Jesus Christ."

Fresh from the battlefields a little band of veterans came forth. To each was given a medal with the names of their battles on one side, and on the other side this little sentence, "I was there. " Oh, when that hour shall come, may it be a supremely happy thought to look back over the trials and sacrifices of these days and remember, "I was there, and by the help of God and the grace of Jesus, I am here."

The fulness of the blessing of the gospel of Christ—Romans 15:29.

Many Christians fail to see all the blessings that are centered in Christ. They want to get the blessing of salvation, but that is not the Christ. They want to get the blessing of His grace to help, but that is not Him. They want to get answered prayer from Him in order to work for Him. You might have all that and not have the blessing of Christ Himself

A great many people are attached to the system of doctrine. They say, "Yes, I have the truth; I am orthodox." That is not the Christ. It may be like the cold statue in the fountain with the water pressing from the cold hands and lips, but having no life.

A great many other people want to get the blessing of joy, but this is not the blessing of Christ personally. Many people become attached to their church and pastor, or to dear Christian friends, but that is not the Christ. The blessing that alone will fill our hearts when all else fails is the loving heart of Jesus united to us, the fountain of all our blessings and the unfailing One when all others wither and are exhausted—Jesus Christ Himself.

Where is the way where light dwelleth
—Job 38:19.

Jewels, in themselves, are valueless unless they are brought into contact with light. If they are put into certain positions they will reflect the beauty of the sun. There is no beauty in them otherwise. The diamond that is stored in a dark gallery or remains down in the deep mine displays no beauty whatever. What is it but a piece of charcoal, a bit of common carbon, unless it becomes a medium for reflecting light?

So it is also with the other precious gems. If they are many-sided, they reflect more light and display more beauty. In its crude state the diamond does not reflect light at all. We are in a crude state and are of no use until God comes and shines upon us. The light that is in a diamond is not its own possession; it is the beauty of the sun. What beauty is there in the child of God? Only the beauty of Jesus. We are His peculiar people, chosen to show forth the excellencies of Him who hath called us out of darkness into His marvelous light (1 Peter 2:9). Let us reflect today His light and love.

That I may know him—Philippians 3:10.

Better to know Jesus Himself than to know the truth about Him, for the deep things of God are revealed to us by the Holy Spirit. Paul's great desire was, *that I may know him.* Not just know about Him, or the mysteries of the wonderful world, or even the deeper and higher teachings of God, but to enter into the Holy of Holies where Christ is, where the Shekinah is shining, making the place glorious with the holiness of God. It is to enter into the secret of the Lord Himself.

It was what Jacob strove for at Peniel when he pleaded with God. God has given us *the light of the knowledge of the glory of God in the face of Jesus Christ* (2 Corinthians 4:6). That is the secret. It is the Lord Himself, and nothing else; it is acquaintance with God; it is knowing Jesus Christ as we know no one else.

It is being able to say not only "I believe Him," but "I know Him." It is being able to say not only "I know about Him," but "I know Him." That is the secret above all others that God wants us to have; it is His provision for glory and power, and it is given freely to the single-hearted seeker.

....

Be careful for nothing; but in every thing by prayer and supplication with thanksgiving let your requests be made known unto God—Philippians 4:6.

C ommit means to hand over, to trust wholly to another. So, if we give our trials to Him, He will carry them. If we walk in righteousness He will carry us through. *Humble yourselves therefore under the mighty hand of God, that he may exalt you in due time* (1 Peter 5:6).

There are two hands there—God's hand pressing us down, humbling us, and then God's hand lifting us up. *[Cast] all your care upon him; for he careth for you* (1 Peter 5:7).

There are two cares in this verse—your care and His care. They are different in the original. One means *anxious* care, the other means *Almighty* care. Cast your anxious care on Him and take His Almighty care instead. No longer be overwhelmed by trouble, but believe God is able to sustain you through it. The government is on His shoulder. Believe that if you trust and obey Him and meet His will, He will look after your interests. Simply exchange burdens. Take His yoke upon you, and let Him care for you.

....

The government shall be upon his
shoulder—Isaiah 9:6.

Y ou cannot make the heart restful by
stopping its beating. Certain drugs will do
that, but that is not really rest. Let the breath of
life come—God's life and strength—and there
will be sweet rest. Home ties and family affection will not bring it. Deliverance from trouble
will not bring it. Many a tried heart has said:
"If this great trouble were only gone, I would
have rest." But as soon as one crisis goes another
comes.

The poor wounded deer on the mountainside
thinks if it could only bathe in the cold mountain
stream it would have rest. But the arrow is in its
flesh, and there is no rest for it until the wound is
healed. It is as sore in the mountain lake as on the
plain.

We shall never have God's rest and peace in
our hearts until we have surrendered everything,
even our work, to Christ and believe He has
taken it all. Then we have only to be still and
trust.

It is necessary to walk in holy obedience and
let God have the government on His shoulder.
Paul said, "This one thing I do." There is one
narrow path for us all—Christ's will and work
for us.

He humbled himself—Philippians 2:8.

One of the hardest things for those having a lofty and superior nature is to be under authority, to renounce their own will and to take a place of subjection. Christ took upon Him the form of a servant, gave up His independence, His right to please Himself, His liberty of choice. After having had from eternal ages the right to command, He gave Himself up to implicit obedience.

I knew a man who was once a wealthy employer but became a clerk in the same store. It was not an easy or graceful position, I assure you.

But Jesus was such a perfect servant that His Father said: *Behold, my servant . . . in whom my soul delighteth* (Isaiah 42:1). All His life His watchword was, *the Son of man came . . . to minister* (Matthew 20:28). *I am among you as he that serveth* (Luke 22:27). *I can of mine own self do nothing* (John 5:30). *Not as I will, but as thou wilt* (Matthew 26:39).

And then at last He became obedient unto death, even the death of the cross. His life was a continual dying, and at last He gave all up to death, and also shame, in His crucifixion. This final act was the consummation of His love.

Have you, have I, learned the servant's place?

The body is . . . for the Lord; and the
Lord for the body—1 Corinthians 6:13.

Just as it was Christ Himself who justified us, and Christ Himself who was made unto us sanctification, so it is only by personal union with Him that we can receive this physical life and redemption. Indeed, it is not a touch of power upon our bodies which restores and then leaves them to the mere resources of natural strength and life for the future. Rather, it is the vital and actual union of our mortal bodies with the risen body of our Lord Jesus Christ, so that His own very life comes into our frames and He is Himself made unto us strength, health and full physical redemption.

He is alive forevermore and condescends to live in these houses of clay. They who thus receive Him may know Him as none ever can who exclude Him from the bodies which He made for Himself. This is one of the deep and precious mysteries of the gospel. *The body is . . . for the Lord; and the Lord for the body. Know ye not that your body is the temple of the Holy Ghost which is in you, . . . and ye are not your own; for ye are bought with a price: therefore glorify God in your body, . . . which [is] God's* (1 Corinthians 6:19-20).

··

I will put my spirit within you
—Ezekiel 36:27.

I *will put my spirit within you, and cause you to walk
in my statutes, and ye shall keep my judgments. I will
put my fear in [your] hearts, that [you] shall not depart
from me* (Jeremiah 32:40). Would you not find
that a blessed rest when you are worn out from
struggling in your own strength? Do you not feel
the need of an invincible man to conquer the
strong man of self and sin? Do you want a leader?
Do you want God Himself to be with you, to be
within you? Do you want rest? Are you conscious of this need?

Are you weary of this sense of being beaten
back, of longing, wanting but not accomplishing? That is what He comes to do. *Ye shall receive
power, after that the Holy Ghost is come upon you*
(Acts 1:8). Better than that, "Ye shall receive the
power of the Holy Spirit coming upon you."
That is the true version, and is immensely different from the other. You shall not receive power
yourself, so that people will say, "How much
power that man has!" You shall not have any
power whatever, but *you shall receive the power of
the Holy Ghost coming upon you.* The power is
His!—and it is sufficient.

....

Whosoever therefore shall humble himself
as this little child—Matthew 18:4.

Y ou will never have a humble heart until it
is born from above, from the heart of
Christ. For man has lost his own humanity and
unfortunately too often has a wicked heart.

God wants us, as Christians, to be simple,
human, approachable and childlike. The Christians who we know and love best, and who are
nearest to the Lord, are the most simple.

Whenever we grow stilted we are fit only for
a picture gallery, or to be placed on a pedestal.
But if we are going to live among men and love
and save them, we must be approachable and
human.

All stiffness is but another form of self-consciousness. Ask Christ for a human heart, for a
smile that will be as natural as your little child's
in your presence.

How much Christ did by little touches! He
never would have reached the woman of Samaria if He had come to her as the prophet. Rather,
He sat down, a tired man, and said, "Give me a
drink of water." And so, all through His earthly
life, it was His simple humanness and love that
led Him to others, and that drew them to Him
and to His great salvation.

That the righteousness of the law might
be fulfilled in us—Romans 8:4.

D o you know the mistake you may be making? You may be saying: "It is not possible
for me to be good; no one ever was perfect, and it
is no use for me to try." I agree with the first
sentence, "No one ever was perfect." But I cannot agree with the second, "There is no use in
trying."

There is a divine righteousness available to
you. I don't mean merely that which pardons
your sins—I believe that, too, but I mean far
more. I mean the righteousness that comes into
your soul and unites itself with the fibers of
your being. I mean Christ—your life, your
purity—who makes you feel as He feels, think as
He thinks, love as He loves, hate as He hates, and
[*partake*] *of the divine nature.* That is God's righteousness—*that the righteousness of the law might be*
fulfilled in us, not *by* us but *in* us.

It is not our hands and feet merely, but our
very instincts, our very desires, our very natures
springing up in harmony with His own. Have
you received Him? He will come and fulfill all
right things in you if today you will open your
heart.

As ye have therefore received Christ
Jesus the Lord, so walk ye in him
—Colossians 2:6.

Here is the very core of spiritual life. It is not a subjective state so much as a life in the heart. Christ for us is the ground of our salvation and the source of our justification; *Christ in us* is the source of sanctification. When this becomes real, [*We*] *are dead.* Our own condition, state and resources are no longer counted upon any more than a dead man's, but . . . [*our*] *life is hid with Christ in God* (Colossians 3:3). It is not even always manifest to us.

Moreover, Christ who is our life must Himself maintain it and be made unto us of God all we need. Therefore, the Christian life is not just coming to Christ to save us, and then going on to work out our own sanctification, but *as* [*we*] *have received Christ Jesus the Lord,* thus to walk in Him, just as dependent and as simply trusting as for our pardon and salvation.

> Ah, friends, how much it would ease
>   our tasks
> For the day that's just begun,
> To live our life a step at a time
> And our moments one by one.

Ye shall receive power, after that the
Holy Ghost is come upon you
—Acts 1:8.

There is power for us if we have the Holy Spirit. God wants us to speak to men so that they will feel it, so that they will never forget it. God means every Christian to be effective, to make a difference in the actual records and results of Christian work. God put each of us here to be a power. There is not one of us but is an essential wheel of the machinery and can accomplish all that God calls us to.

There is not a thing that God expects of a person but that God will give him or her the power to do. There is not a command God gives to His children for which He does not provide the enablement for obedience. When Christ Jesus lived and died and sent down the Holy Spirit, He sent resources for all our needs, and there is no place for failure in the Christian life if we will take God's resources. Jesus, the ascended One, and the Holy Spirit, the indwelling energy, life and efficiency of God are sufficient for all possible emergencies. Do you believe this? If you believe it, let Him into your heart, without reserve, and allow Him to control you and work through you today by His power.

Looking unto Jesus—Hebrews 12:2.

There must be a constant looking unto Jesus, or, as the German Bible states it, an off-looking upon Jesus—that is, looking off from the evil, refusing to see it, not letting the mind dwell upon it for a second. We should have mental eyelids as well as physical ones, which can be used like shields to keep out evil. They should be like a stockade camp in the woods, to repel the first assault of the enemy.

Many do not seem to know that they have spiritual eyes. They go through the world as if somebody had cut off their eyelids. The devil comes along with his evil pictures and bids them look, and they stare away at the good and evil alike.

We cannot look upon evil without being defiled. Sometimes, as we walk along the streets, the sight of some of the pictures will cast their filth upon our souls so that we feel the need of being cleansed in Jesus' blood. There has been no consent unto sin, but the sight of it has defiled us. The only remedy is in the resolute, steady, inner view of Christ.

Trust ye in the Lord for ever—
Isaiah 26:4.

Trial is the fruitful soil of trust. Difficulties are the divine incentives which
demand and develop our confidence in the divine
faithfulness and love. The eagle can only teach
her young by tearing up her nest and hurling
them out in mid-air, where, thrown upon their
own resources, they must either fly or fall. As
they strike out upon the air in desperate struggles, they find the secret of a new life and grad-
ually learn to beat their way through the pathless
firmament.

So God teaches His children to use the wings
of faith by stirring up their nests, taking away
their props and often flinging them out into an
abyss of helplessness, where they must either sink
or learn to trust. They throw themselves upon
the seeming void to find that God is there beneath them like the supporting wing which the
eagle stretches forth beneath her faint and faltering brood.

It is so easy for us to lean upon the things that
we can see and feel that it is an entirely new
experience for us to stand alone and walk with
the unseen God. . . . But it is a lesson we must
learn if we are ever to dwell in the eternal realm,
where faith shall be our only sense and God shall
be our All in all.

He humbled himself—Philippians 2:8.

The first step to the righteousness of the kingdom is *poor in spirit*. The next is a little deeper, *they that mourn*. Because now we must become pliable, we must be broken, we must be like the metal in the fire which the Master can mold. It is not enough to see our unrighteousness, but deeply to feel it, deeply to regret it, deeply to mourn over it, to consider it no little thing that sin has come into our lives.

And so God leads us into His righteousness. He usually leads us through testings and trials. I do not think it necessary for us to have deep and great suffering before we are saved. He will put us into the fire when He knows we are saved, when we realize we are accepted, when we are not afraid of the discipline, when we know it is not the hand of wrath but the hand of love. Then God can take us down and make us poor in spirit, and make us mourn until we come to the third step, which is to be *meek,* broken, yielded, submissive, willing, surrendered and laid low at His feet crying, "What wilt thou have me to do?"

When ye go, ye shall not go empty
—Exodus 3:21.

When we are really emptied He delights to fill us with Himself and the Holy Spirit. It is very precious to be conscious of nothing good in ourselves; but are we also conscious of His great goodness? We may be ready to admit our own disability, but are we as ready to admit His ability? There are many Christians who can say, "I am not *sufficient of [myself] to think any thing as of [myself];* . . . but the number is very small who can say, *[My] sufficiency is of God* (2 Corinthians 3:5).

Are you convinced that He is able to provide every want in you, or do you feel that you must supply it yourself? Do you believe that God does supply every lack in your heart and life, so that all stumbling is taken away and you are endowed with power for His service?

Our Savior, at Cana, ordered the waterpots to be filled to the brim. Then the water was made into wine, but not until the vessels were full. God wants His children always to have a full heart.

Bread corn is bruised—Isaiah 28:28.

The farmer does not gather timothy and bluegrass and break it with a heavy machine. But he takes severe measures to separate the kernals of wheat. So God takes great pains with those who are to be of much use to Him. There is a nature in them that needs this discipline. Do not wonder at God's wise, discriminating care that will fit them to be food for the multitude.

God knows the way He is taking, and there is infinite tenderness in the oversight He gives. He is watching the furnace you are in; He will not allow the heat to become too intense. He wants it great enough to purify and then it will be withdrawn. He knows our frame. He will not let any temptation take us *but such as is common to man: but God is faithful, who will not suffer you to be tempted above that ye are able; but will with the temptation also make a way to escape, that ye may be able to bear it* (1 Corinthians 10:13).

Do you believe in this disciplining love of the Heavenly Husbandman? Are you trusting Him with the leading and government of your life? Do not permit yourself to envy or be disturbed by the people around you! Some day you will be glad for the training and blessing they have brought you.

> *Ye are the light of the world*
> *—Matthew 5:14.*

We are called the lights of the world—light bearers, reflectors, candlesticks, lamps. We are to be kindled ourselves, and then we will burn and give light to others.

We are the only light the world has. The Lord could come down Himself and give light to the world, but He has chosen differently. He wants to send it through us, and if we do not give it the world will not have it. God does not put a meteor in the sky to tell us when to shine. We are to be giving light continually wherever we are—at home, among friends or in church. We should have the attitude that we may never have another opportunity, and so we should always be shining for Him. Let our lamps be trimmed and full of the oil of the Spirit. Above all, let us be a *steady* light to those without Christ.

> Let me dwell in Timnath-serah,
> Where the sun forever shines.
> Where the night and darkness come not,
> And the day no more declines.

Your heavenly Father knoweth ye have need—Matthew 6:32.

Christ makes no less of our trust for temporal things than He does for spiritual things. He places much emphasis upon it. Why? Simply because it is harder to trust God for material needs. In spiritual matters we can fool ourselves and think that we are trusting when we are not; but we cannot do so about rent and food and the needs of our bodies. They must come or our faith fails. It is easy to say that we trust Him in things that are a long way off, but there can be no question about it where faith must bring practical answers.

When the sun is shining, it is easy to have faith for our needs and to trust God. But let something arise which irritates and rasps and frets us, and we soon find whether we have real trust or not. Consequently, the things of everyday life are tests of our real faith in God, and He often puts us where we have to trust for tangible matters— for money and rent, food and clothes. If in these things you are not trusting God wholly, you will break down when you are placed in such tests. Are you trusting God for everything?

....

Thou hast the dew of thy youth
—Psalm 110:3.

O h, that we might get such a view of Him as would make it impossible for little things ever to fret us again! The petty cares that have troubled us so much ought rather to cause us to wonder that we can think so much about them.

If we had the dew of His youth we would go forth as the morning and fulfill the promise of a glorious day! What a difference it would make in life were we to realize this is possible! How easy it would be, when the little troubles come, to draw a little closer to Christ, to drink in a little more of that fountain of life, to get a little nearer to that loving heart and to draw in great draughts of refreshing and strength from it. How clear it would make the head for work!

Coming to Him thus, heavy and dull and tired, we can become rested and able to spring forth ready for work. How inspiring to think that our living Head never grows weary! He is as fresh as He ever was. He is a glorious conqueror. He is ever the victorious Christ. Let Him take you today, and He will cause you to see in Him the invincible Leader!

··

We would see Jesus—John 12:21.

Glory to Jesus for all the things laid up for us in the days to come. Glory to Him for all the visions of service in the future, the opportunities of doing good that are far away as well as close at hand.

Our Savior was able to despise the cross for the joy that was before Him. Let us look up to Him, and rise up to Him until we reach the peak and are able to look out from the mount of vision over all the distant land. Not a single thing will come to us in all the future in which we may not be able to see the King in His beauty. Let us be very sure that we look at nothing else. Our pupils will then become so impressed as they look at this vision that they will not be able to reflect anything else.

My small son came to me once and said, "Papa, look for a long time at that golden sign across the street. Now look at that brick wall and tell me what you see."

"Why, I see the yellow sign on the brick wall," I replied. And he laughed merrily over it.

So, if we look a long time upon Jesus we cannot look at anything else without seeing a reflection of Him. Everything which we behold will become a part of Him.

The sweetness of the lips increaseth learning—Proverbs 16:21.

Life is made up very largely of words. They are not so emphatic, perhaps, as deeds, for deeds are more deliberate expressions of thought. Yet one of the most remarkable authors of the New Testament said, *If any man offend not in word, the same is a perfect man* (James 3:2). Not offending in word is often a test of victory in the Christian life. Our triumph in this often depends on both what we say and what we do not say.

Speaking of the tongue, James said, *It is set on fire of hell.* The true Christian, therefore, is righteous in his ways and upright in his words. His deeds appeal to men; and in speech he is looking up, for God is listening. His words are sent upward and recorded for the judgment.

I can almost imagine that the beautiful blue sky over our heads, seemingly so transparent, is like a wax tablet with a finely sensitive surface which receives an impression of every word we speak, and that these tablets are then hardened and preserved for the eternal judgment. We should speak with our eyes ever upward, never forgetting that we shall some day meet the words that we have spoken.

The secret of the Lord is with them that fear him—Psalm 25:14.

There are secrets of providence which God's dear children may learn. His dealing with them often seems, to the outward eye, dark and terrible. Faith looks deeper and says, "This is God's secret. You look only on the outside; I can look deeper and see the hidden meaning." Sometimes diamonds are hidden in rough packages so their value cannot be seen.

When the tabernacle was built in the wilderness there was nothing rich in its outside appearance. The costly things were all within, and its outward covering of rough badger skin gave no hint of the valuable things which it contained. God may send you some costly packages. Do not worry if they are concealed in rough wrappings. You may be sure there are treasures of love and kindness and wisdom hidden within.

Do not be so foolish as to throw away a silver spoon because it is tarnished. If we take what He sends, and trust Him for the goodness in it, even in the dark, we shall learn the meaning of the secrets of His providence.

Grow up into him in all things
—Ephesians 4:15.

Harvest is a time of ripeness. Then the fruit and grain are fully developed, both in size and weight. Time has tempered the acid of the green fruit. It has been mellowed and softened by the rains and the heat of summer. The sun has tinted it into rich colors, and at last it is ready and ripe to fall into the hand.

So the Christian life ought to be. There are many things in life that need to be mellowed and ripened. Many Christians have orchards full of fruit, but the fruit is green and sharp to the taste. There is a great deal in these Christians that is good, but it is incomplete—very sharp and sour. Perhaps something goes wrong in their domestic lives. They become flustered and cross and lose their confidence in God, and then, of course, their Christian joy. These things produce regret and all kinds of misery.

Every day there are things for which we are sorry. We know we are not ripe and mellow and that we cannot become so by trying. We cannot bring the sweetness in. It must be wrought out from within.

....

Ye cannot serve God and mammon
—Matthew 6:24.

Jesus does not say you cannot very well serve God and mammon. Rather, He says you cannot serve two masters at all. If you try, you will surely end up serving only one. The person who thinks he or she is serving God a little is deceived. He or she is not serving God. God will not have that service. The devil will monopolize the person before long.

A divided heart loses both worlds. Saul tried it. Balaam tried it. Judas tried it. Their efforts ended in desperate failure.

For Mary there was but one choice. Paul said: *This one thing I do,* and *For me to live is Christ.* Of such a life God says: *Because he hath set his love upon me, therefore will I deliver him: I will set him on high, because he hath known my name* (Psalm 91:14). God takes a peculiar pride in revealing His love to the heart that wholly chooses Him. Heaven and earth will fade away before its trust can be disappointed. Have we chosen Him only and given Him all our hearts?

> Say, is it all for Jesus,
> As you so often sing?
> Is He your Royal Master?
> Is He your heart's dear King?

The glory of the Lord shall be thy rereward—Isaiah 58:8.

He comes by our side as our helper. More than that, He comes to dwell within us, to be the life in our blood, the fire in our thought, the faith within us, both in inception and consummation. Thus He becomes not only the recompense of the victor, but the resources of the victory. He is the Captain, the Overcomer and the Rear Guard in our lives.

The help that relieved us on that particularly troubled morning—it was of Him. He lifts our eyes up unto Himself and delivers us from apathy, from discontent and from fears. He is always the helper in this heavenly competition and will be the great reward in all the ages to come.

If our life is hidden with Him we shall have to go through the same trials that He went through, but we shall not find them too hard. If we but take Him fully as the strength of our life, and our all in all, we shall be able to lay aside all the hindering things that press upon us day by day.

> I have overcome, overcome,
> Overcome for thee.
> Thou shalt overcome, overcome,
> Overcome thro' Me.

....

I am doing a great work, so that I
cannot come down—Nehemiah 6:3.

When work is pressing, there are many little things that will come and seem to need attention. It is a very blessed thing to be quiet and still, work on and entrust the little things to God. He answers such trust in a wonderful way. The believer who has no time to fret and worry and harbor care has learned the secret of faith in God. A desperate desire to change some difficult circumstance may take our eyes off God and His glory. Some suffering Christians have been so anxious to get well and have spent so much time in trying to claim healing, that they have lost their spiritual blessing. God sometimes has to teach such persons that there must be a willingness to be sick before they are yielded enough to receive His fullest blessing.

The enemy keeps at this work. Sanballat came four times to Nehemiah, always receiving the same answer. How many fears we have stopped to fight which ultimately have proved to be nothing. Nehemiah recognized that fear is sin and did not dare to yield to it.

Who hath first given to him, and it
shall be recompensed unto him again
—Romans 11:35.

Christians have it in their power, by a very
little sacrifice, to add millions to the
treasury of the Lord. Have you found the joy of
sacrifice for Jesus? Have you given up something
that you might give it to Him? Are you giving
your substance to Jesus? He will take it, and will
return to you a thousandfold.

I would rather be associated with a work
founded on great sacrifice than on enormous en-
dowments. The reason God loved the place
where His ancient temple rose in majesty was
because there Abraham offered his son and
David his treasure. The reason redemption is so
dear to the Father and the heavenly world is because its foundation stone is the cross of Calvary.

The Christian life that is dearest to the heart
of God, and that will rise to the highest glory and
usefulness, is the one whose foundation principle
is sacrifice and self-renunciation. This is why the
Master teaches us to give—because giving means
loving, and love is but another name for life.

....

Let every man abide in the same
calling wherein he was called
—1 Corinthians 7:20.

Do you complain about your calling or fret about the changes and trials of life? How do you know but that these very changes are the divine methods by which God's purposes of blessing and usefulness concerning you are being fulfilled?

Had Aquila and Priscilla not been compelled to leave Rome and break up their home and business, they probably would never have met Paul, nor would they have come to know and serve Christ through this providential meeting. Had they not been working persons pursuing their ordinary vocation, they would not have been brought into contact with the apostle. It was in the line of their calling, their common duties and the providential changes of their lives that God called them. And so He meets us.

Do not attempt to run away from your calling, but, as the apostle has so aptly put it, *Let every man wherein he is called, therein abide with God* (1 Corinthians 7:24). Make the most of your incidental opportunities.

> *God hath set some in the church . . . helps*
> —*1 Corinthians 12:28.*

In the Apostle's lists of officers in the church, the *helps* are mentioned before the *governments*. By the ministry of prayer, by the ministry of giving, by the ministry of encouragement, by the shining face and mute pressure of the hand and a little word of cheer, and by the countless ways in which we can help—or at least can keep from hindering—we can all still find the footprints of Aquila and Priscilla, if we want to follow them.

It is a valuable gift to be able to rejoice in another's work and pour our lives, like affluent streams, into great rivers. But God knows the source of every drop, and in the greater day of recompense many of the *helps* shall have the chief reward.

Are you helping? Are you helping your pastor, your brother, your husband, your mother, your father, your fellow worker? And when the harvest comes shall not *he that soweth and he that reapeth rejoice together?*

> You can help by holy prayer,
> Helpful love and joyful song,
> Oh, the burdens you may bear,
> Oh, the sorrows you may share,
> Oh, the crowns you yet may wear,
> If you help along.

....

This is that bread which came down from heaven—John 6:58.

*W*e had the sentence of death in ourselves, that we should not trust in ourselves, but in God which raiseth the dead: who delivered us from so great a death and doth deliver: in whom we trust that he will yet deliver us* (2 Corinthians 1:9). This was the supernatural secret of Paul's life; he drew continually in his body from the strength of Christ, his Risen Head.

The body that came out of Joseph's tomb was to him a physical reality and the inexhaustible fountain of his vital forces. More than the other apostles he has imparted to us the secret of his strength. *We are members of his body, of his flesh, and of his bones* (Ephesians 5:30). *The body is . . . for the Lord; and the Lord for the body* (1 Corinthians 6:13).

Marvelous truth! Divine elixir of life and fountain of perpetual youth! Earnest of the resurrection! Fulfillment of the ancient psalms and songs of faith! *The Lord is the strength of my life; of whom shall I be afraid?* (Psalm 27:1). *My flesh and my heart faileth: but God is the strength of my heart, and my portion forever* (Psalm 73:26). Have we learned this secret, and are we living the life of the Incarnate One in our flesh?

*Now are we the sons of God, and it
doth not yet appear what we shall be*
—*1 John 3:2.*

We are the sons of God. We are not
merely called such or even legally de-
clared so, but we actually *are* sons of God by receiving the life and nature of God. And so we are
the very brethren of our Lord, not only in His
human nature, but still more so in His divine relationship.

Therefore, he is not ashamed to call [*us*] *brethren*
(Hebrews 2:11). He gives us that which entitles
us to that right, and makes us worthy of it. He
does not introduce us into a position for which
we are uneducated and unfitted, but He gives us
a nature worthy of our glorious standing; and as
He shall look upon us in our complete and glorious exaltation—reflecting His own likeness and
shining in His Father's glory—He shall have no
cause to be ashamed of us.

Even now He is pleased to acknowledge us
before the universe and call us brethren in the
sight of all earth and heaven. Oh, how this digni-
fies the humblest saint of God! How little we
need mind the misunderstanding of the world if
He *is not ashamed to call* [*us*] *brethren.*

So let us go out today to rightly represent His
royal family.

I will clothe thee with change of raiment—Zechariah 3:4.

For Paul every exercise of the Christian life was simply the grace of Jesus Christ imparted to him and lived out by him. To be holy meant to put on the Lord Jesus and all the robes of His perfect righteousness which Paul describes so often in his beautiful letters.

Put on therefore, as the elect of God, holy and beloved, he says to the Colossians, *bowels of mercies, kindness, humbleness of mind, meekness, long suffering* and *above all these things put on love, which is the bond of perfectness* (Colossians 3:12). None of these things is regarded as an intrinsic quality in us. Rather, they are all imparted graces from the hand of Jesus. And even in the later years of life, and after the mature experience of a quarter of a century, we find Paul exclaiming, *I count all things but loss for the excellency of the knowledge of Christ Jesus my Lord: for whom I have suffered the loss of all things, and do count them but refuse, that I may win Christ, and be found in him* (Philippians 3:8-9).

Lord, enable us today to go out, clothed in Thy robes of perfect rightness, and with our hearts in adjustment with Thy perfect love.

....

[Who] always causeth us to triumph
—2 Corinthians 2:14.

E very victor must first be a self-conqueror.
But the method of Joshua's victory was the
uplifted arm of Moses on the mount. As Moses
held up his hands, Joshua prevailed; as he low-
ered them, Amalek prevailed. It was to be a battle of faith and not of human strength. The banner that was to wave over the discomfited foe
was *Jehovah-nissi.* This, too, is the secret of our
spiritual triumph. If we are led of the Spirit we
shall not fulfill the lust of the flesh (Galatians 5:16).
*Sin shall not have dominion over you: for ye are not under
the law, but under grace* (Romans 6:14).

Have we begun the battle and in the strength
of Christ planted our feet on our own necks? And
thus victorious over the enemy in the citadel of
the heart, have we been set at liberty for the
battle of the Lord and the service of others? It
was this lack that hindered the life of Saul, and it
has wrecked many a promising career. One enemy in the heart is stronger than ten thousand in
the field. May the Lord lead us all into Joshua's
first triumph and show us the secret of self-
crucifixion through the greater Joshua, who
alone can lead us on to holiness and victory!

···

When he saw the multitudes he was
moved—Matthew 9:36.

He is able to be *touched with the feeling of our infirmities* (Hebrews 4:15). The word "touched" is very expressive. It means that our troubles are His troubles, and that in all our afflictions He is afflicted. It is not a sympathy of sentiment, but a sympathy of suffering.

There is in this thought abundant help for the tired heart. It is the foundation of Christ's Priesthood, and God meant that it should be to us a source of unceasing consolation. Let us realize more fully our oneness with our Great High Priest, and cast all our burdens on His great heart of love.

If we know what it is to ache in every nerve with the responsive pain of our suffering child, we can form some idea of how our sorrows touch the heart of Christ. As the mother feels her baby's pain, as the heart of friendship echoes every cry from another's anguish, so in heaven our exalted Savior, even in the raptures of that happy world, is suffering in His spirit and even in His flesh with all that His children bear. *Seeing then that we have a great high priest, . . . let us therefore come boldly to the throne of grace* (Hebrews 4:14,16) and let us come to our Great High Priest.

··

Be filled with the Spirit—Ephesians 5:18.

S ome of the effects of being filled with the
Spirit are:

1.   Holiness of heart and life. This is not the perfection of the human nature, but the holiness of
the divine nature dwelling within.

2.   Fullness of joy so that the heart is constantly
radiant. This does not depend on circumstances,
but fills the spirit with holy laughter in the midst
of the most trying surroundings.

3.   Fullness of wisdom, light and knowledge,
causing us to see things as He sees them.

4.   An elevation, improvement and quickening
of the mind by an ability to receive the fulfillment of the promise, *We have the mind of Christ*
(1 Corinthians 2:16).

5.   An equal quickening of the physical life. The
body as well as the mind and soul was made for
the Holy Spirit.

6.   An ability to pray the prayer of the Holy
Spirit. If He is in us there will be a strange
accordance with God's working in the world
around us.

Leaning upon her beloved
—Song of Solomon 8:5.

Will we make the claim most practical and real and, like John, at the Last Supper, lean our full weight upon our Lord's breast? That is the way He would have us prove our love. "If you love me lean hard," said a heathen woman to her missionary, as she was timidly leaning her tired body upon her stalwart body. She felt slighted by the timorous reserve and asked the confidence that would lay all its weight upon the one she trusted.

Jesus says to us, [*Cast*] *all your care upon* [*me*]; *for* [*I care*] *for you* (1 Peter 5:7). He would have us prove our love by a perfect trust that makes no reserve. He is able to carry all our care, to manage all our interests, to satisfy all our needs.

Let us go forth leaning upon Him and feeding on His life. For John not only leaned but also fed. It was at supper that he leaned. This is the secret of feeding on Him, to rest upon His bosom. This is the need of the fevered heart of man. Let us cry to Him, *Tell me, O thou whom my soul loveth, where thou feedest, where thou makest thy flock to rest at noon* (Song of Solomon 1:7).

....

*He dwelleth with you, and shall be in
you—John 14:17.*

Do not fail to mark these two stages in
Christian life. The one is the Spirit's work
in us, the other is the Spirit's personal coming to
abide within us. All true Christians know the
first, but few, it is to be feared, understand and
receive the second.

There is a great difference between my building a house and my going to reside in that house
and making it my home. And there is a great
difference between the Holy Spirit's work in re-
generating a soul—the building of a house—and
His coming to reside, abide and control in our
innermost spirit and our whole life and being.

Have we received Him, not as our Guest, but
as the Owner, Proprietor and Keeper of the
temple He has built to be *an habitation of God
through the Spirit?* (Ephesians 2:22).

> This is my wonderful story,
> Christ to my heart has come,
> Jesus the King of glory
> Finds in my heart a home.
>
> I am so glad I received Him,
> Jesus my heart's dear King,
> I, who so often have grieved Him,
> All to His feet would bring.

....

Therefore, choose—Deuteronomy 30:19.

Men are choosing every day the spiritual or earthly. And as we choose we are taking our place unconsciously with the friends of Christ or the world. It is not merely what we say; it is what we prefer.

When Solomon made his great choice at Gibeon, God said to him, *Because this was in thine heart . . . to ask wisdom, . . . wisdom and knowledge is granted unto thee; and I will give thee riches, and wealth, and honour, such as none of the kings have had that have been before thee* (2 Chronicles 1:11-12). It was not merely that he said it because it was right to say and would please God if he said it. But it was the thing his heart preferred, and God saw it in his heart and gave it to him, along with riches, wealth and honor that he had not chosen.

What are we choosing? It is our choice that settles our destiny. It is not how we feel, but how we purpose. Have we chosen the good part? Have we said, "Whatever else I am or have, let me be God's child; let me have His favor and blessing; let me please Him"? Or have we said, "I must have this thing, and then I will see about religion"? Alas, God has seen what was in our hearts, and perhaps He has already said, "They have their reward."

After that ye have suffered a while
—1 Peter 5:10.

Are we learning love in the school of suffering? Are our hearts being mellowed and deepened by the summer heat of trial until the fruit of the Spirit—love, joy, peace, longsuffering, gentleness, goodness, faith, meekness, temperance—is ripening for the harvest of His coming, and our sufferings are easily borne for His sake? This is the school of love, and the lessons make Him unutterably more dear to our hearts and us to His. In this way only can we learn with Him the heavenly charity which suffers long, and is kind.

We see that the very first and the very last features of the face of love, as delineated in Paul's portrait of it (1 Corinthians 13), are marks of pain and patient suffering—*suffers long, endureth all things*. So let us learn in the school of love to suffer, to be kind and to endure all things.

Surely it will not be hard to love through every circumstance when it is the heart of Jesus within us that will love and continue to love to the very end.

> I want the love that suffers and is kind,
> That envies not nor vaunts its pride
> of fame.
> Is not puffed up, does not
> discourteous act,
> Is not provoked, nor seeks its own
> to claim.

And hath raised us up together
—Ephesians 2:6.

Ascension is more than resurrection. Much is said of it in the New Testament. Christ rises above all things. We see Him in the very act of ascending, as we do not in the actual resurrection. With hands and lips engaged in blessing, He gently parts from His disciples. So simply, so unostentatiously, He has brought heaven near to our common life.

We, too, must ascend, even here. *If ye then be risen with Christ, seek those things which are above* (Colossians 3:1). We must learn to live on the heavenly side and look at things from above.

To contemplate all things as God sees them, as Christ beholds them, overcomes sin, defies Satan, dissolves perplexities, lifts us above trials, separates us from the world and conquers fear of death. Such a perspective enables us to view them as we shall one day look back upon them from His glory, and as if we were now really seated with Him, as indeed we are, in heavenly places (Ephesians 2:6).

Let us arise with His resurrection and, in fellowship with His glorious ascension, learn to live above.

Look from the top
—Song of Solomon 4:8.

Yes, our perplexities would become plain if we kept on a spiritual elevation. Often when the traveler quite loses his way he can discern it again from some hilltop where all the winding paths on which he has come appear behind him, and the whole homeward road opens before. So, from the heights of prayer and faith, we too can see the plain path and know we are going home.

There is no other way in which we can gain the victory over the world. We must rise above it. We must see it from the side of our great reward. Then it will look like earthly objects do after we have gazed upon the sun for a while. We are blind to them.

When the Italian fruit seller finds that he is heir to a ducal palace you cannot tempt him anymore with the paltry profits of his trade or the company of his old associates. He is above it all. They who know the hope of their calling and the riches of the glory of their inheritance can well despise the world. It is the poor starving ones who go hungering for the husks of earth. We are born from above and have a longing to go home. Let us go forth today with our hearts on the home stretch.

Whosoever abideth in him sinneth not
—1 John 3:6.

What becomes of our old nature when we are sanctified? Many people are unduly concerned to know if it can be killed outright and seem to desire a sort of certificate of its death and burial. It is enough to know that it is outside and Christ is in us. It may show itself again, and even knock at the door and plead for admittance, but it is forever outside while we abide in Him. Should we step out of Him and into sin we might find the old corpse in the ghastly cemetery, and its foul aroma might yet embrace and overcome us once more. But he that *abideth in him sinneth not* and cannot sin while he so abides.

Let us therefore abide and let us not be anxious to escape the hold of eternal vigilance and ceaseless abiding. Our paths are made and we are given strength to pursue them; let us then walk in them. God has provided for us a full sanctification. Since He has given us His own holiness, is it strange that he should require us to be holy, even as He is holy? Let us then put on our beautiful garments and prepare to walk in white with Him.

A garden enclosed—Song of Solomon 4:12.

The figure here is of a beautiful, fruitful enclosure, not a wilderness. Garden soil is cultivated soil, very different from the roadside or wilderness. The idea of a garden is culture. The ground has to be prepared, to be broken up by ploughing, to be mellowed by harrowing. All the stones have to be removed and the roots of all natural growth dug up. The good things we are seeking are not natural growths and will not prosper in our natural soil. We all feel we should try to improve the old nature, but that is not God's way. His method is to get self out of the way entirely, and let Him create anew out of nothing, so that all shall be of Him; and Jesus will be the acknowledged Alpha and Omega.

The thing we want to learn here is to die. There can be no real life till self dies. And we dare not try to die ourselves, but ask God to slay us; He will make a thorough work of it.

> This the secret nature hideth,
> Summer dies and lives again,
> Spring from winter's grave ariseth,
> Harvest grows from buried grain.

If the household be too little for the lamb, let him and his neighbour next unto his house take it according to the number of the souls—Exodus 12:4.

If the household be too little for the lamb. . . . What does all this mean for us as redeemed men and women? Surely, this—that we have no right to claim the purchase of the Savior's blood for ourselves alone, and that we are guilty of selfishness, dishonesty and base ingratitude if we can be content to be saved without having done everything in our power to give our fellow men an equal opportunity of eternal life. Have we understood this? Have we lived it?

But who is the neighbor with whom we are to share God's Lamb? He is spoken of here as the one that is next to us, the one in closest contact with us. Surely, that means that God brings people into touch with us in order that we may be stewards of His grace to them. The people in our families, the fellow traveler, friends in our social circles and people with whom we work— these are the neighbors to whom we owe a spiritual responsibility. Have we met it according to our utmost ability?

> Did'st Thou love and die for
> A sinner like me?
> Then, Master, I will take
> More thought for the perishing
> Souls I may meet
> If it's only for Thy sake.

And the glory of the Lord filled the tabernacle—Exodus 40:35.

In the last chapter of Exodus we read of all the Lord commanded Moses to do. As he fulfilled these commands the glory of the Lord descended and filled the tabernacle until there was no room for Moses. From that time the pillar of cloud overshadowed the tabernacle as Israel's guide and their protection.

Even so we have been building as the Lord Himself commanded, and now the temple is to be handed over to Him, to be possessed and filled. He will so fill us, if we will let Him, that self and everything else will be taken out of the way. The glory of the Lord will fill the temple, encompassing, lifting, guiding, keeping; and from this time our moon shall not withdraw its light, nor our sun go down.

Do you want power? You have God for it. Do you want holiness? You have God for it. You have God for every need! He is bending down from His throne today to lift you to your true place in Him. From this time on may the cloud of His glory so surround and fill us that we shall be lost sight of forever.

Having begun in the Spirit, are ye
now made perfect by the flesh
—Galatians 3:3.

Grace literally means that which we do not have to earn. It has two great senses always; it comes without charge, and it comes when we are helpless. Grace does not merely help the man who helps himself—that is not the gospel. The gospel is that God helps the man who cannot help himself. In addition, God helps the man to help himself, for everything the man does comes from God. Grace is given to the man who is so weak and helpless he cannot take the first step. That is the meaning of grace—at least a little of its meaning. We can never know the fullness of it.

This river of grace is as free as it is full, but some people, surprisingly, have the idea that when they get a little farther on they must pay an admission, or pay to reserve a seat, and they shrink back from the higher blessings of the gospel. Ordinary Christians scarcely dare to claim them. If I understand the meaning of the gospel, God has not put the higher blessings apart for a separate class who somehow are nearer to Him. God is no respecter of persons.

Cast thy burden on the Lord
—Psalm 55:22.

Sometimes when we bring a burden to God, we do so much groaning over it that it seems as though God is having a dreadful time, too. In reality it does not burden Him at all. God says in effect, "It is a light thing for Me to do this for you." Our load, though heavy for us, is not heavy for Him. Christ carries the whole on one shoulder, not two shoulders. The government of the world is upon His shoulder, and He is not struggling and groaning with it. His mighty arm is able to carry all our burdens.

There is power in Christ for our sanctification. Yes, the Lord can sanctify, the Lord can heal, the Lord can do anything. You must have faith in God. If you come to a river this morning, will it take you as the mighty Niagara would take a little boat and carry you along—to a precipice? Oh, no, but to the heart of love and blessing forever.

> Oft there comes a wondrous message,
> When my hopes are growing dim,
> I can hear it thro' the darkness
> Like some sweet and far-off hymn.
> Nothing is too hard for Jesus
> No man can work like Him.

That we might know the things that
are freely given to us of God
—1 Corinthians 2:12.

The highest blessings of the gospel are just as free as the lowest; when you have served God ten years you cannot sit down and say, "I have an experience now and I count on that." We so often do that! We say, "Now I know I am saved, I feel it." And so we are building a different foundation—we build on something in ourselves.

Always take grace as something you do not deserve, something that is freely bestowed. The long, deep, boundless river is free—as free at the mouth as it is at the little feeder stream. It is free all along its course; anybody can come and drink, and anybody can come and bathe in its refreshing waters. Do you believe that?

God has given us His Holy Spirit that we may *know the things that are freely given to us of God.* It is a sad thing for a poor starving child to look longingly through the window and see a fire and the happy family sitting around a laden table. What is the good of knowing that there is warmth and love and light if it is not free? God has freely given all the goodness of His grace and love.

For it is God which worketh in you
—Philippians 2:13.

A day with Jesus. Let us seek its plan and direction from Him. Let us take His highest thought and will for us in it. Let us look to Him for our desires, ideals, expectations in it. Then it will bring to us the *exceeding abundantly above all that we ask or think* (Ephesians 3:20). Let Him be our Guide and Way. More even than thinking of His plan and way, let us think of Him as our personal every-moment Guide, on whom we constantly depend to lead us step by step.

Let Him also be the sufficiency and strength for all the day. Let us never forget the secret: *I can do all things through Christ which strengtheneth me* (Philippians 4:13). Let us have Jesus Christ Himself in us to do the works, and let us every moment depend on Him, *both to will and do* [*in us*] *of his good pleasure* (Philippians 2:13). Let our holiness be *the law of the Spirit of life in Christ Jesus* (Romans 8:2). Let our health be the *life . . . of Jesus . . . manifest in our mortal flesh* (2 Corinthians 4:11). Let our faith be *the faith of the Son of God, who loves* [*us*] (Galatians 2:20). Let our peace and joy be His peace and joy. And let our service be not our works, but the grace of Christ within us.

....

When ye pray, believe that ye receive
—Mark 11:24.

Consecration is entered into by an act of faith. We are to take sanctification as a gift from God, believing and confessing that we have it. We must step out on it firmly. We must let the devil also know we have it. When once we tell the Lord, boldly, "I am yours," He answers back from the heavenly heights, "You are Mine," and the echoes go ringing down through all our lives, "Mine!" "Yours!"

If you dare confess Christ as your Savior and Sanctifier, He has bound Himself to make these truths a reality. But you must stand behind His mighty Word. It is the essence of testimony to tell what Jesus has promised to become to you. It is right to have a glorious word of testimony. God would have us put our seal on the promises and lift up our hands and acknowledge them as ours.

Then you are to ignore the old life and reckon it no longer yours—even if it should return to trouble you again. Every time it appears say, "This is from the underworld. I am sitting in the heavenly places with Christ."

Even Christ pleased not himself
—Romans 15:3.

L et this be a day of self-forgetting ministry for Christ and others. Let us not once think of being ministered unto, but rather say with Him: *I am among you as he that serveth* (Luke 22:27). Let us not drag our burdens through the day but drop all our loads of care and be free to carry His yoke and His burden. Let us make the happy exchange, relinquishing ours and taking His. Let the covenant be: *Thou shalt abide for me . . . so will I also be for thee* (Hosea 3:3).

In such abiding we lose our heaviest load—ourselves—and find our highest joy, divine love, *more blessed to give than to receive* (Acts 20:35). Let us do good to all men as we have opportunity. Let us lose no occasion of blessing, and let us look for ingenious ways of service and usefulness. Especially let us seek to win others to Christ.

> The Days of Heaven are busy days,
> They serve continually.
> So spent for Thee and Thine, our days,
> As the Days of Heaven would be.

Men ought always to pray
—Luke 18:1.

Let this be a day of prayer. Let us realize that our highest ministry and power is to deal with God for men. Let us be obedient to all the Holy Spirit's voices of prayer in us. Let us consider every pressure a call to prayer. Let us cultivate the spirit of unceasing prayer and constant communion.

Let us learn the meaning of the ministry of prayer. Through prayer let us reach people this day whom we cannot reach in person. Let us expect results that we have never dared to claim before. Let us count every difficulty only a greater occasion for prayer. And let us call on God, who will show us many great and mighty things which we know not.

And let this also be a day of joy and praise. Let us live in the promises of God and the expectancy of His deliverance and blessing. Let us never dwell on the trial but always on the victory just ahead. Let us not abide in the tomb, but in the garden of Joseph and the light of the resurrection. Let us keep our faces toward the rising sun. *Arise, shine. Rejoice evermore. In everything give thanks. Praise ye the Lord.*

Lord, give us Thy joy in our hearts which shall lift us to lift others, and fill us so we may overflow to others.

*I am my beloved's, and my beloved is
mine—Song of Solomon 6:3.*

If I am the Lord's then the Lord is mine. If
Christ owns me I own Him. And so faith must
reach out and claim its full inheritance and begin
to use its great resources. Moment by moment
we may now take Him as our grace and strength,
our faith and love, our victory and joy, our all in
all. And as we thus claim Him we will find His
grace sufficient for us, and begin to learn that
giving all is just receiving all.

Consecration is taking Jesus fully in exchange
for our own miserable lives. There are two persons involved in such consecration. One of them
is the Lord Himself. *And for their sakes,* He says,
*I sanctify myself, that they also might be sancti-
fied through the truth* (John 17:19). The moment
we consecrate ourselves to Him, He consecrates Himself to us. Thereafter the whole
strength of His life and love and everlasting
power is dedicated to keep and complete
our commitment to Him and to make the very
best and most of our consecrated lives. Who
would not give himself to such a Savior? Today, let us first give ourselves to
Jesus, and then present to Him each moment
as it comes, to be filled and used.

As the hart panteth after the water brooks, so panteth my soul after thee, O God—Psalm 42:1.

In order to enter into a life of consecration, there must be a sense of need—the need of purity, of power and of a greater nearness to the Lord. Christians often experience a second conviction. It is not now a sense of guilt and God's wrath so much as of the power and evil of inward sin, and the dissatisfaction with the life the person is living. It usually comes from the deeper revelation of God's truth, from more spiritual teaching, from definite examples and testimonies of this life in others. Or it may result from an experience of deep trial, conflict and temptation in which the Christian has found his attainments and resources inadequate for the real issues and needs of life.

The first result is often a deep discouragement and even despair, but the Valley of Achor is the door of hope, and Romans 7 with its bitter cry, *O wretched man that I am* (7:24) is the gateway to Romans 8 with its shout of triumph, *The law of the Spirit of life in Christ Jesus hath made me free from the law of sin and death* (8:2).

....

By one offering he hath perfected
forever them that are sanctified
—Hebrews 10:14.

Are you missing what belongs to you? Jesus has promised to sanctify you. He has promised sanctification for you by coming to you Himself and being made of God to you sanctification. Jesus is our sanctification. Having Him, we have obedience, rest, patience and everything we need. He is alive forevermore.

If you have Jesus nothing can be against you. Your temptations will not be against you. Your bad temper will not be against you. Your hard life, your circumstances—even the devil himself will not be against you. Every time he comes to attack you, he will only root you deeper in Christ. You will become a coward at the thought of being alone; you will be thrown on Jesus every time a trouble confronts you. From now on, all things will work together for good to your spiritual welfare. Since God is for you nothing can be against you.

> My heavenly Bridegroom sought me
>   and called me one glad day.
> "Arise, my love, my fair one,
>   arise and come away,"
> I listened to His pleading, I gave Him
>   all my heart,
> And we are one forever
>   and nevermore shall part.

Ye are complete in him
—Colossians 2:10.

In Jesus we are now complete. Even as the architect's model is planned and prepared and completed in his office, so the perfect pattern of the life of holy service, for which Jesus has redeemed and called us, is now in Him in heaven.

But now it must be formed in us and transferred to our earthly lives, and this is the Holy Spirit's work. He takes the gifts and graces of Christ and brings them into our lives as we need and receive them day by day, just as the various sections of a vessel may be reproduced in a distant land. Thus we receive of His fullness, even grace for grace—His grace for our grace, His supply for our needs, His strength for our strength, His body for our body, His Spirit for our spirit. He Himself *of God is made unto us wisdom, and righteousness, and sanctification, and redemption* (1 Corinthians 1:30).

But it is much more than mere abstract help and grace, much more even than the Holy Spirit bringing us strength, and peace and purity. It is personal companionship with Jesus Himself!

Lord, help us receive from Thee today that grace in all trials that shall result in our being made perfect.

Nevertheless, David took the castle of Zion—1 Chronicles 11:5.

If you seem to have so much fighting to do, it may be because you did not have one sharp, decisive battle to begin with. It is far easier to have one great battle than to keep on skirmishing all your life. I know men who spend forty years fighting what they call their besetting sin, and on which they waste strength enough to evangelize the world.

Does it pay to throw away your lives? Why not have one battle, one victory and then praise God. There is labor to enter in. The height is steep; the way of the cross is not an easy way. It is hard to enter in, but having entered in, there is perfect rest. *And when he giveth you rest from all your enemies round about* (Deuteronomy 12:10). May God help us and give us His perfect rest.

> O come, and leave thy sinful
>   self forever
> Beneath the fountain of
>   the Saviour's blood;
> O come, and take Him as
>   thy Sanctifier,
> Come thou with us and we will
>   do thee good.

....

Let us also go, that we may die
with him—John 11:16.

Let us also go, that we may die with him—this was
an outburst of impetuous love from the
heart of Thomas. The disciples had been trying
to dissuade the Master from going back to Judea
because of the hate which the raising of Lazarus
had aroused and the certainty of danger if He
should return. But when Thomas saw that their
persuasions did not avail and that Jesus was certainly going back to face His enemies, he cried in
an impulse of desperation and devotion, "Let us
also go, that we may die with him." Thomas's
cry was that of a devoted soldier ready to follow
his leader into the jaws of danger and death.

Thomas's words were wiser than he knew. It
is true that he and his fellow disciples did not
immediately share their Master's fate, but there
was a deep and sacred sense in which they were
to die with Him even before their literal perse-
cution and martyrdom.

In a very real and solemn way, these words are
true of every disciple of Christ. For His death is
not only the source of our salvation, but it is also
the pattern of our lives.

With an intelligent faith and a renewed dedi-
cation, let us with Thomas, "also go that we may
die with Him."

Look from the place where thou art
—Genesis 13:14.

L et us think for a moment of the blessed-ness of faith. Our own littleness and nothingness sometimes becomes bondage. We are so small in our own eyes we dare not claim God's mighty promises. We say: "If I could be sure I was in God's will I could trust."

This is all wrong. Self-consciousness is a great barrier to faith. Get your eyes on Him and Him alone. Not on your faith, but on the Author of your faith; not with a half look, but with a stead-fast, prolonged look, with a true heart and fixed-ness of purpose that knows no faltering, no par-leying with the enemy and not a shadow of fear. When you become fearful you are almost sure to fail.

Travelers who have crossed the Alps know how dangerous those mountain passes are, how narrow the foothold, how deep the rocky ra-vines. They know how necessary to safety it is that they look up continually. One downward glance into the dizzying depths might be fatal. So if we would surmount the heights of faith we must look up—look up. Take your eyes off your-self, off surrounding circumstances, off means, off gifts, and turn them to the Great Giver.

Or ministry, let us wait on our ministering—Romans 12:7.

Beloved, are you ministering to Christ? Are you doing it with your hands? Are you doing it with your substance and with your gifts? Is He getting the best at your table? And when He does not come to fill the chair, is it free to His representative, His poor and humble children? Your words and wishes are cheap if they do not find expression in your actual gifts. Even Mary did not put Him off with the incense of her heart. Rather, she laid her costliest gift at His feet.

Busy person, you who work so hard to dress your children and furnish your home and table, what have your hands earned for the Master? What have you done or sacrificed for Jesus?

"Can you afford it?" was the question asked of an earnest woman as she promised a costly offering for the Master's work.

"No," was her noble reply, "but I can sacrifice it."

Let us today look around us and see what we are presently doing. Then let us give more to the loving Savior, who gave up His whole life for us.

Bring them hither to me—Matthew 14:18.

Why have you not received all the fullness of the Holy Spirit? Do you not long to be anointed with *the rest of the oil?* (Leviticus 14:17-18). Look around you at your situation. Are you not conscious of many needs at this very moment and almost overwhelmed with difficulties, trials and emergencies? These are all divinely provided vessels for the Holy Spirit's filling. If you would only understand their meaning, they will become opportunities for receiving new blessings and deliverances which you can obtain in no other way.

Bring these vessels to God. Hold them steadily before Him in faith and prayer. Keep still. Cease your own restless working until He begins to work. Do nothing that He does not Himself command you to do. Give Him a chance to work, and He will surely do so. Then the very trials that threatened to overcome you with discouragement and disaster will become God's opportunity for the revelation of His grace and glory in your life, as you have never known Him before. *Bring them [all needs] to me.*

That the righteousness of the law
might be fulfilled in us—Romans 8:4.

In our earlier experiences we know the Holy
Spirit only at a distance, in things that happen
in a providential direction or in the Word alone.
But after a while we receive Him as an inward
Guest, and He dwells in our hearts. He speaks to
us in the innermost chambers of our being. The
external working of His power does not cease;
rather, it increases and seems even more glorious. The Power that dwells within us works outside us, answering prayer, healing sickness,
overruling providences, doing *exceeding abun-*
dantly above all that we ask or think, according to the
power that worketh in us (Ephesians 3:20).

There is a double presence of the Lord for the
consecrated believer. He is present in the heart
and is mightily present in the events of life. He is
the Christ in us and the Christ of all our days,
with all power in heaven and earth.

The Holy Spirit is our wonder-worker, our
all-sufficient God and Guardian. And He is waiting in these days to work as mightily in the affairs
of men as in the days of Moses, of Daniel and of
Paul.

*He that in these things serveth Christ
is acceptable to God—Romans 14:18.*

God can only use us while we are trusting Him completely. Satan cared far less for Peter's denial of his Master than for the use he made of it afterwards to destroy his faith. So Jesus said to him, *I have prayed for thee that thy faith fail not* (Luke 22:32). It was Peter's faith Satan attacked, and so it is our faith that he contests. *The trial of your faith, being much more precious than of gold that perisheth* (1 Peter 1:7).

Whatever else we let go, let us hold steadfastly to our trust. *Cast not away therefore your confidence* (Hebrews 10:35), and *hold fast the confidence and rejoicing of the hope firm unto the end* (Hebrews 3:6). And if you would hold your trust, hold your sweetness, your rightness of spirit, your obedience to Christ, your victory in every way.

Whatever comes, regard it as of less consequence than that you should triumph and remain steadfast. Accept every circumstance as something God is pleased to allow. Wave the banner of your victory in the face of every foe. Go on, shouting in Jesus' name, *Thanks be unto God, which always causeth us to triumph in Christ* (2 Corinthians 2:14).

....

Now mine eyes seeth thee—Job 42:5.

We must recognize the true character of our self-life and its real virulence and vileness. We must consent to its destruction, and we must take it ourselves, as Abraham did Isaac, and lay it at the feet of God in willing sacrifice.

This is a seemingly impossible task for the natural heart, but the moment the will is yielded and the choice is made, we are astonished to find that the agony is over and death is accomplished.

Usually the crisis in such cases hangs upon a single point. God does not need to strike us in a hundred places to inflict a death wound. There is one point that touches the heart, and that is the point God usually strikes. It will likely be the dearest thing in our lives, the decisive thing in our plans, the citadel of our wills, the center of our hearts. And when we yield there, there is little left to yield anywhere else. But when we refuse to yield at that point, a spirit of evasion and compromise enters into all the rest of our lives. Let us take Him to enable us to will His will in all things in our lives.

Unto the measure of the stature of the fullness of Christ—Ephesians 4:13.

God is preparing His heroes. When the opportunity comes He can fit them into their places in a moment, and the world will wonder where they came from. Let the Holy Spirit prepare you by all the discipline of life. When the last finishing touch has been given to the marble, it will be easy for God to put it on the pedestal and fit it into its niche.

There is a day coming, when, like Othniel (see Judges 3:9-11) we too shall judge the nations and rule and reign with Christ on the millennial earth. Before that glorious day can be, we must let God prepare us as He did Othniel at Kirjath-Sepher (Judges 1:11-13) amid the trials of our present life and in the little victories the significance of which, perhaps, we little dream. We may be sure of this, that if the Holy Spirit has an Othniel ready, the Lord of heaven and earth has a throne prepared for him.

> Is it for me to be used by His grace,
> Helping His kingdom to bring?
> Is it for me to inherit a place,
> E'en on the throne of my King?

Not my will, but thine—Luke 22:42.

Jesus who once suffered in Gethsemane will be our strength and our victory, too. We may fear, we may also sink, but let us not be dismayed, and we shall yet praise Him and look back from a finished course and say, *Not one thing hath failed of all the good things which the Lord* [*our*] *God spake concerning* [*us*] (Joshua 23:14).

But in order to do this, we must, like Jesus, meet the conflict, not with a defiant but with a submissive spirit. He had to say, *Not my will, but thine be done,* but in saying it He gained the very thing He surrendered. The submission of Gethsemane is not a blind and dead submission of a heart that abandons all its hope, but it is the free submission that bows the head in order to get double strength through faith and prayer.

We let go in order that we may take a firmer hold. We give up in order that we may more fully receive. We lay our Isaac on Mount Moriah, and we receive him back, no longer *our* Isaac, but *God's* Isaac and infinitely more secure because he is returned to us in resurrection life.

My helpers in Christ Jesus
—Romans 16:3.

Christ's Church is overrun with captains. It is in great need of a few more privates. A few rivers run into the sea, but a larger number run into other rivers. We cannot all be pioneers, but we can all be helpers. No man is fitted to go in first place until he has learned well how to go second.

A spirit of self-importance is fatal to all work for Christ. The biggest enemy of true spiritual power is spiritual self-consciousness. Joshua had to die to human plans and strategy before Jericho could fall.

God often has to test His chosen servants by putting them into a subordinate place before He can bring them to the front. Joseph had to learn to serve in the kitchen and to suffer in prison before he could rise to the throne. As soon as he was ready for the throne, the throne was waiting for Joseph. God has more places than accepted candidates. Let us not be afraid to go into the training class and even take the lowest place, for we shall soon move up if we really deserve to.

Lord, use me so that Thou shalt be glorified and I shall be hidden from myself and others.

If thou wilt diligently hearken unto the voice of the Lord thy God, . . . and wilt keep all his statutes—Exodus 15:26.

Sometimes people fail because they lack confidence in the Physician. The very first requirement for your healing is that you trust the Physician, and trust Him implicitly—so implicitly that you go forward on His bare word and act as if you had received His healing the moment you claimed His promise.

You must also do what the Great Physician tells you, if you expect Him to make you whole. The pills prescribed by your doctor would do you no good if left on the cupboard shelf.

You cannot expect to be healed if you are living in sin, any more than you could expect the best physician to cure you while you lived in a malarial climate or inhaled poison with every breath. So you must move from doubt into the pure air of trust and obedience before Christ can make you whole. And then if you will trust Him and respond to His directions, you will find that there is balm in Gilead and a Great Physician there.

....

We were troubled on every side
—2 Corinthians 7:5.

Why should God have to lead us through troubles and allow the pressure to be so hard and constant?

In the first place, it shows His all-sufficient strength and grace much better than if we were exempt from pressure and trial. *We have this treasure in earthen vessels, that the excellency of the power may be of God, and not of us* (2 Corinthians 4:7).

Also, it makes us more conscious of our dependence upon God. God is constantly trying to teach us our dependence and to hold us absolutely in His hand and hanging upon His care.

This was the place where Jesus Himself stood and where He wants us to stand, not with a self-constituted strength, but with a hand ever leaning upon His, and a trust that dares not take one step alone.

Troubles teach us trust. There is no way of learning faith except by trial. It is God's school of faith, and it is far better for us to learn to trust God than to escape trials.

The lesson of faith, once learned, is an everlasting acquisition and an eternal fortune made. Without trust even riches will leave us poor.

> *For we must all appear before the judg-*
> *ment seat of Christ; that every one*
> *may receive the things done in his*
> *body, according to that he hath*
> *done—2 Corinthians 5:10.*

It will not always be the day of toil and trial. Some day we shall hear our names announced before the universe and the record read of things that we had long forgotten. How our hearts will thrill, and our heads will bow, as we hear our own names called, and then the Master shall recount the triumph and the services which we had ourselves forgotten! And, perhaps, from the ranks of the saved He shall call forward the souls that we have won for Christ, and the souls that they in turn have won. As we see the issue of things that have, perhaps, seemed unimportant at the time, we shall fall before the throne, and say, *Not unto us, O Lord, not unto us, but unto thy name give glory* (Psalm 115:1).

Beloved, each day we are adding pages to the record of our lives. We are setting the type ourselves, by every moment's action. Soon the record will be read before the audience of the universe and amid the issues of eternity.

Thy gentleness hath made me great
—Psalm 18:35.

The blessed Comforter is gentle, tender and full of patience and love. How gentle are God's dealings even with sinners. How patient His forbearance. How tender His discipline with His own erring children. How He led Jacob, Joseph, Israel, David, Elijah and all His ancient servants until they could truly say, *Thy gentleness hath made me great.*

The heart in which the Holy Spirit dwells will always be characterized by gentleness, lowliness, quietness, meekness and forbearance. The rude, sarcastic spirit, the brusque manner, the sharp retort, the unkind cut—all of these belong to the flesh and have nothing in common with the gentle teaching of the Comforter.

The Holy Dove shrinks from the noisy, tumultuous, excited and vindictive spirit and finds His home in the peaceful soul. *The fruit of the Spirit is . . . gentleness, . . . meekness.*

Lord, make me gentle. Hush my spirit. Refine my manner. Let me have Christ in my bearing and my very tones, as well as in my heart.

Humble yourselves therefore under
the mighty hand of God
—1 Peter 5:6.

The pressure of hard places makes us value life. Every time we come through such a trial, it is like a new beginning, and we learn better how much life is worth and make more of it for God and man. The pressure helps us to understand the trials of others and fits us to help and sympathize with them.

There is a shallow, superficial nature that gets hold of a theory or a promise and talks very glibly about the distrust of those who shrink from every trial. But the man or woman who has suffered much never does this. Knowing what suffering really means, he or she is very tender and gentle.

This is what Paul meant when he said, *Death worketh in us, but life in you* (2 Corinthians 4:12). Trials and hard places are needed to press us forward, even as the furnace fires in the hold of the mighty steamship give the force that moves the piston, drives the engine and propels that great vessel in the face of winds and waves.

*Ye are not in the flesh, but in the
Spirit, if so be that the Spirit of God
dwell in you. Now if any man have
not the Spirit of Christ, he is none
of his—Romans 8:9.*

A spiritual man is not so much a man possessing a strong spiritual character as a man
filled with the Holy Spirit. So the apostle Paul
said: *Ye are not in the flesh, but in the Spirit, if so be
that the Spirit of God dwell in you.*

The glory of the new creation, then, is not
only that it recreates the human spirit, but that it
fits it for the abode of God Himself, and makes it
dependent upon the Son, as the child upon the
mother. The highest spirituality, therefore, is
the most utter helplessness, the most total
dependence and the most complete possession of
the Holy Spirit. The beautiful act of Christ in
breathing upon His disciples and imparting to
them from His own lips the very Spirit that was
already in Him expressed in the most vivid manner the crowning glory of the new creation. And
when the Holy Spirit thus possesses us, He fills
every part of our being.

....

If any man hear my voice, and open the
door, I will come in to him, and will sup
with him, and he with me
—Revelation 3:20.

Some of us are starving and wondering why the Holy Spirit does not fill us. We have plenty coming in, but we do not give it out. Give out the blessing you have, start larger plans for service and blessing and you will soon find that the Holy Spirit is before you. He will *prevent [precede] you with blessings of goodness* (Psalm 21:3) and give you all that He can trust you to give away to others.

There is no music so heavenly as an Aeolian harp. The Aeolian harp is nothing but a set of stretched strings arranged in harmony and then left to be touched by the unseen fingers of the wandering winds. As the breath of heaven floats over the chords, notes almost divine float out upon the air as if a choir of angels were wandering around and touching the strings.

And so it is possible to keep our hearts so open to the touch of the Holy Spirit that He can play upon them at will, as we quietly wait in the pathway of His service.

> *As many as are led by the Spirit of*
> *God, they are the sons of God*
> *—Romans 8:14.*

The blessed Holy Spirit is our Guide, our Leader and our Resting-place. There are times when He presses us forward into prayer, into service, into suffering, into new experiences, new duties, new claims of faith and hope and love. Then there are times when He arrests us in our activity and rests us in the secret place of the Most High. He teaches us some new lessons, breathing into us some deeper strength or fullness and then leading us on again, at His bidding alone.

The Holy Spirit is the true Guide of the saint, and the true Leader of the Church. He is our wonderful Counselor, our unerring Friend. He who would deny the personal guidance of the Holy Spirit in order that he might honor the Word of God as our only guide must dishonor that other word of promise, that His sheep shall know His voice, and that His listening and obedient children *shall hear a voice behind them saying, this is the way, walk ye in it* (Isaiah 30:20).

Knowing this, that our old man is
crucified—Romans 6:6.

It is purely a matter of faith. Faith and sight always differ. To your senses it does not seem to be so, but your faith must still reckon it so. This is a very difficult attitude to hold, and only as we thoroughly believe God can we thus reckon upon His Word and His working. But as we do so, faith will convert it into fact, and it will become reality.

These two words "yield" and "reckon" are passwords into the resurrection life. They are like the two edges of the "Sword of the Spirit" through which we enter into crucifixion with Christ.

This act of surrender and this reckoning of faith are recognized in the New Testament as marking a very definite crisis in the spiritual life. It does not mean that we are expected to be going through a continual dying, but that there should be one very definite act of dying, and then a constant habit of reckoning ourselves as dead and meeting everything from this standpoint.

Reckon ye also yourselves to be dead indeed unto sin, but alive unto God through Jesus Christ our Lord (Romans 6:11).

> *If any man offend not in word, the same is a perfect man, and able also to bridle the whole body—James 3:2.*

S peech is one of the supreme distinctions between man and the lower animals. The power of expressing thought in articulation and written language is one of the high prerogatives of rational beings.

A man's conversation is the real test of his character and *if any man among you seem to be religious, and bridleth not his tongue, but deceiveth his own heart, this man's religion is vain* (James 1:26). An unbridled tongue is a sure sign of an unsanctified spirit. On the other hand, *if any man offend not in word, the same is a perfect man, and able also to bridle the whole body.* It is a sign that he is under the government of his conscience, his will and the Holy Spirit. This is a most heart-searching test.

It was a foolish word that lost Moses the Land of Promise. He would have taken it back if he could have, but it was too late. Though he was taken to heaven, he could not lead Israel into the promised land.

Many men and women of great potential ruin their whole lives by an uncontrolled tongue. It settles our character and influence here. How much more in the sight of Him who has said, *By thy words thou shalt be justified and by thy words thou shalt be condemned* (Matthew 12:37).

Aaron shall lay both his hands upon the head of the live goat, and confess over him all the iniquities of the children of Israel—Leviticus 16:21.

As any evil comes up and the consciousness of any unholy thing touches our inner senses, it is our privilege at once to hand it over to the Holy Spirit and to lay it upon Jesus as something already crucified with Him. Then, as was done with the sin offering, it will be carried outside the camp and burned to ashes.

There may be deep suffering, there may be protracted pain, and it may be intensely real; but throughout all there will be a very sweet and sacred sense of God's presence, of intense purity in our whole spirit and of our separation from the evil which is being consumed. Truly, it will be borne outside the camp, leaving not even the smell of the flames upon our garments.

It is so blessed to have the Holy Spirit slay things. No sword but His can pass so perfectly between us and the evil, so that it consumes the sin without touching the spirit.

Lord Jesus, my sin offering, I lay my sin, myself, my whole nature, upon Thy cross. Consume me by Thy holy fire, and let me die to all but Thee!

There is no spot in thee
—Song of Solomon 4:7.

The blessed Holy Spirit who possesses the consecrated heart is intensely concerned for our highest life and watches us with a sensitive and even a jealous love. Very beautiful is the true translation of that ordinary passage in James 4:5, *The Spirit that dwelleth in us loveth us to jealousy.*

The heart of the Holy Spirit is deeply concerned in preserving us from every stain and blemish and in bringing us into the very highest possibilities of the will of God.

The heavenly Bridegroom would have His Church not only free from every spot, but also from every *wrinkle, or any such thing.* The spot is the mark of sin, but the wrinkle is the sign of weakness, age and decay; Jesus wants no such defacing touch upon the holy features of His beloved. So the Holy Spirit, who is the Executor of His will and the Divine Messenger whom He sends to call, separate and bring home His Bride, is jealously concerned in fulfilling in us all the Master's will.

Lord, take from me every blemish and mark of weakness and decay and make me Thy spotless Bride.

All the land which thou seest
—Genesis 13:15.

The actual provisions of God's grace come from the inner vision.

He who gives to the bird the instinct to cross the continent in search of summer sunshine in a southern climate is too good to deceive it. And just as surely as He has put the instinct in the breast of the bird, so has He also put the balmy breezes and the vernal sunshine there to meet it when it arrives.

He who gave to Abraham the vision of the Land of Promise also said in infinite truth and love: *All the land that thou seest will I give thee.* He who breathes into our hearts the heavenly hope will not deceive or fail us when we press forward to its realization. There is nothing unfaithful in Him who has said: *If it were not so, I would have told you* (John 14:2), and we may know that God never will deceive us or fail us, but all that He reveals by His Holy Spirit He will make our own as we press forward and enter into its realization.

Lord, give me first the vision and then the victory. Show me all my inheritance, and then give it all to me in Christ Jesus.

Not ourselves, but Christ Jesus
—2 Corinthians 4:5.

Your Christian influence, your reputation as a worker for God and your standing among your brethren may be an idol to which you must die before you can be free to live for Jesus alone.

If you have ever noticed the type on a printed page, you must have seen that the little "i" always has a dot over it. It is that dot that elevates it above the other letters in the line.

Now, each of us is a little i, and over every one of us there is a little dot of self-importance, self-will, self-interest, self-confidence, self-complacency—or something to which we cling and for which we contend. But it just as surely reveals self-life as if it were a mountain of real importance.

This *i* is a rival of Jesus Christ. It is the enemy of the Holy Spirit and of our peace and life. God has therefore decreed its death, and the Holy Spirit, with His flaming sword, is waiting to destroy it that we may be able to enter through the gates and come to the Tree of Life.

Lord, crowd me out by Thy fullness, even as the glory of the Lord left no room for Moses in the tabernacle.

Clouds and darkness are round about him—Psalm 97:2.

The presence of clouds upon your sky and trials in your path are the very best evidence that you are following the pillar of cloud and walking in the presence of God. The disciples had to enter the cloud before they could behold the glory of the transfiguration. A little later that same cloud became the chariot to receive the ascending Lord, and it is still waiting as the chariot that will bring His glorious appearing.

Still it is true that while *clouds and darkness are round about him,* mercy and truth are ever in their midst and *shall go before thy face* (Psalm 89:14).

Perhaps the most beautiful and gracious use of the cloud was to shelter Israel from the fiery sun. Like a great umbrella, that majestic pillar spread its canopy above the camp and became a shielding shadow from the burning heat in the treeless desert. One who has never felt an oriental sun cannot fully appreciate how much this means—a shadow from the heat.

So the Holy Spirit comes between us and the fiery, scorching rays of sorrow and temptation.

*Touch not mine anointed, and do my
prophets no harm—Psalm 105:15.*

I would rather play with the forked lightning
than to speak a reckless word against any
servant of Christ. I would rather take in my
hands live wires with their fiery current than
to idly repeat the slanderous darts which thousands of Christians are hurling at others to the
hurt of their own souls and bodies.

You may wonder why your sickness is not
healed, why your spirit is not filled with the
joy of the Holy Spirit, why your life is not
blessed and prosperous. It may be that some
dart which you have flung with angry voice
or in an idle hour of thoughtless gossip is
pursuing you on its way. It is describing the
circle which always brings back to the source
from which it came every shaft of bitterness
and every idle and evil word.

Let us remember that when we persecute or
hurt the children of God, we are but persecut-
ing Him and hurting ourselves far more.

Lord, make me as sensitive to the feelings
and rights of others as I have often been to my
own, and let me live and love like Thee.

He will guide you into all truth
—John 16:13.

The Holy Spirit does not come to give us extraordinary manifestations but to give us life and light. The nearer we come to Him the more simple will His illumination and leading be. He comes to *guide* [*us*] *into all truth.* He comes to shed light upon our own hearts and to show us ourselves. He comes to reveal Christ, to give, and then to illumine the Holy Scriptures and to make divine realities vivid and clear to our spiritual apprehension. He comes as a Spirit of wisdom and revelation in the knowledge of Christ, to enlighten the eyes of our understanding, that we *may know what is the hope of his calling, and what the riches of the glory of his inheritance in the saints, and what is the exceeding greatness of his power to us-ward who believe, according to the working of his mighty power* (Ephesians 1:18-19).

> Spirit of Power! with heavenly fire,
> Our souls endue, our tongues inspire;
> Stretch forth Thy mighty hand,
> Thy Pentecostal gifts restore,
> The wonders of Thy power once more
> Display in every land.

I am with you alway—Matthew 28:20.

Oh, how it helps and comforts us in the plodding of life to know that we have with us the Christ who spent the first thirty years of His life swinging a hammer in the carpenter shop at Nazareth, covered with sweat and grimy dust, physically weary as we often are, and able to understand all our experiences of drudgery and labor! Moreover, He still loves to share our common tasks and equip us for our difficult undertakings of hand and brain.

Yes, housewife, He will help you at the kitchen range and sink as gladly as at the hour of prayer. Yes, busy laborer, He will go with you and help you to swing the hammer, or handle the saw, or hold the plow in the soil of life. You will be a better mechanic, a more skilled workman, a more successful man because you take His wisdom for the common affairs of life.

There is no place or time where Jesus is not able and willing to walk by our side, to work through our hands and minds, and to unite Himself in loving and caring partnership with all our needs and tasks and trials. In this way He proves Himself our all-sufficiency for all things.

Speak ye unto the rock—Numbers 20:8.

The Holy Spirit is very sensitive, as love always is. You can conquer a wild beast by blows and chains, but you cannot conquer a woman's heart that way, or win the love of a sensitive nature; that must be wooed by the delicate touches of trust and affection. So the Holy Spirit has to be taken by a faith as delicate and sensitive as the gentle heart with whom it is coming in touch. One thought of unbelief, one expression of impatient distrust or fear will instantly check the perfect freedom of His operations as much as a breath of frost would wither the petals of the most sensitive rose or lily.

Speak to the Rock, do not strike it. Believe in the Holy Spirit and treat Him with the most tender confidence and unwavering trust, and He will meet you with instant response and confidence.

Have you come to the rock in Kadesh? (Numbers 20:1-8). Have you opened all your being to the fullness of the Spirit, and then, with the confidence of the child to the mother, the bride to the husband, the flower to the sunshine, have you received by faith, and are you drinking of His blessed life?

The three hundred blew the trumpets
—Judges 7:22.

We little dream sometimes what a hasty word, a thoughtless speech, an imprudent act, or a confession of unbelief and fear may do to hinder our highest usefulness or turn it aside from some great opportunity which God has been preparing for us.

Although the Holy Spirit uses weak men, He does not want them to be weak after He chooses and calls them. Although He uses the foolish things to confound the wise, He does not want us to be foolish after He comes to give us His wisdom and grace. He uses the foolishness of preaching, but not necessarily the foolishness of preachers. Like the electric current which can supply the strength of a thousand men, it is necessary that it should have a proper conductor, and a very small wire is better than a very big rope.

God wants fit instruments for His power—wills surrendered, hearts trusting, lives consistent and lips obedient to His will. Then He can use the weakest weapons and make them mighty through God to the pulling down of strongholds.

....

Have faith in God—Mark 11:22.

God requires of us a perfect faith, and He tells us that if we believe and doubt not, we shall have whatsoever we ask. The faintest touch of unbelief will neutralize our trust.

But how shall we have such perfect faith? Is it possible for human nature? No, but it is possible to the divine nature; it is possible to the Christ within us. It is possible for God to give us faith, and He does. But Christ is the Author and Finisher of our faith, and He bids us have the faith of God. As we have faith through the imparting of the Spirit of Christ, we believe even as He.

We pray in His name and in His very nature, and, [*we*] *live by the faith of the Son of God, who loved* [*us*], *and gave himself for* [*us*] (Galatians 2:20). The love that He requires of us is not mere human love, or even the standard of love required in the Old Testament, but something far higher. The *new commandment* is to *love one another* (John 13:34), not as ourselves, but as He has loved us.

How shall such love be made possible? *Our* love is simply *His* love working in us and imparted to us through the Spirit.

Herein is my Father glorified—John 15:8.

The true way to glorify God is for God to show His glory through us, to shine through us as empty vessels, reflecting His fullness of grace and power.

The sun is glorified when it has a chance to show its light through the crystal window, or in reflection from the spotless mirror or the glassy sea.

There is nothing that glorifies God so much as for a weak and helpless man or woman to be able to triumph through His strength in places where the highest human qualities will fail us and to carry on in divine power through every form of toil and suffering. A spirit naturally weak, irresolute, selfish, and sinful, transformed into sweetness, purity and power and standing victorious amid circumstances from which its natural qualities must utterly unfit it brings glory to God. A mind not naturally wise or strong, yet directed by a divine wisdom and carried along the path of a great and mighty plan, being used to accomplish stupendous results for God and man—this glorifies God.

Father, let me glorify Thee this day and adorn Thy doctrine in all things I do.

The battle is not yours
—2 Chronicles 20:15.

The thing is to count the battle God's. *The battle is not yours but God's.* We shall not need to fight in this battle. As long as we count our dangers and responsibilities, we shall be distracted with fear. But when we realize God is bound to take care of us as His property and His representatives, we shall feel infinite relief and security.

If I send my employee on a long journey, I am responsible for his expenses and protection; if God sends me anywhere, He is responsible. If we belong to God and put our life, our family, and our all in His hands, we may know He will take care of us.

If our body belongs to God, it is His interest to keep us well, just as much as it is for the interest of the shepherd to have his sheep well fed, well cared for and a credit to him.

Thanks be unto God, which always causeth us to triumph (2 Corinthians 2:14).

Stand up, stand up for Jesus,
Stand in His strength alone;
The arm of flesh will fail you,
Ye dare not trust your own.

I the Lord, the first, and with the last
—Isaiah 41:4.

Thousands of people get stranded after they have embarked on the great voyage of holiness because they have depended upon the experience rather than on the Author of it. They had supposed that they were thoroughly and permanently delivered from all sin, and in the ecstasy of their first experience they imagined that they never would be tried and tempted as before.

When, therefore, they step out into the actual facts of Christian life and find themselves failing and falling, they are astonished and perplexed, and they conclude that they must have been mistaken in their experience. Then they make a new attempt at the same thing, and again fall, until at last, worn out with the experiment, they conclude that the experience is a delusion, or at least that it was never intended for them. Thus they fall back into the old way, and their last state is worse than the first.

Men and women today need to know not sanctification as a state but Christ as a living Person.

Lord Jesus, give me Thy heart, Thy faith, Thy life, Thyself.

Even as he is pure—1 John 3:3.

God is now aiming to reproduce in us the pattern which has already appeared in Jesus Christ, the Son of God. The Christian life is not an imitation of Christ, but a direct new creation in Christ, and the union with Christ is so complete that He imparts His own nature to us and lives His own life in us. This, then, is not an imitation but simply the outgrowth of the nature implanted within.

We live Christlike because we have the Christ-life. God is not satisfied with anything less than perfection. He required that from His Son. He requires it from us, and He does not, in the process of grace, reduce the standard, but He brings us up to it. He does not let down the righteousness of the law, but He requires of us a righteousness that far exceeds the righteousness of the scribes and Pharisees, and then He imparts it to us. He counts us righteous in sanctification, and He says of the new creation, *He that doeth righteousness is righteous, even as he is righteous* (1 John 3:7).

Lord, live out Thy very life in me.

Let your moderation be known unto
all men—Philippians 4:5.

The very test of consecration is our willingness not only to surrender the things that are wrong, but to surrender our rights, to be willing to be subject. When God begins to subdue a soul, He often requires us to yield the things that are of little importance in themselves and thus breaks our necks and subdues our spirits.

No Christian worker can ever be used of God until the proud self-will is broken and the heart is ready to yield to God's every touch, no matter through whom it may come.

Many people want God to lead them in their way, but they will endure no authority or restraint. They will give their money, but they want to dictate how it shall be spent. They will work as long as you let them please themselves, but let any pressure come and you immediately run up against not the grace of resignation but a letter of resignation. They may withdraw from some important trust, and arouse a whole community of criticizing friends, who are equally disposed to have their own opinions and their own way. Such attitudes are destructive of all real power.

And I will put my spirit within you,
and cause you to walk in my statutes,
and ye shall keep my judgments, and
do them—Ezekiel 36:27.

This state spoken of by Ezekiel is much more than a new heart. It is a heart filled with the Holy Spirit, the Divine Spirit, the power that causes us to walk in God's commandments.

This is the greatest crisis that comes to a Christian: when into the spirit that was renewed in conversion, God Himself comes to dwell, to make it His abiding place, and to hold it by His mighty power in holiness and righteousness.

After this occurs, one would suppose that we would be lifted up into a much more hopeful and exuberant spirit, but the prophet gives a very different picture. He says when this comes to pass we shall loathe ourselves in our own eyes.

The revelation of God conveys a profound sense of our own nothingness and worthlessness and lays us on our face in the dust in self-denial. The incoming of the Holy Spirit displaces self and disgraces self forever. The highest holiness is to walk in self-renunciation.

Thine handmaid hath not anything in the house, save a pot of oil—2 Kings 4:2.

Elisha asked the widow, "What hast thou in the house?" And she said, "Nothing but a pot of oil." But that pot of oil was adequate for all her needs, had she only known how to use it. In truth it represented the Holy Spirit, and the great lesson of the incident is that the Holy Spirit is adequate for all our needs, if we only know how to use Him.

All the widow needed was to get sufficient vessels to hold the overflow, and then to pour out until all were filled. Even so the Holy Spirit is limited only by our capacity to receive Him, and when God wants us to have a larger fullness, he has to make room for it by creating greater needs.

God sends us new vessels to be filled with His Holy Spirit in the needs that come to us and the trials that meet us. These are God's opportunities to give us more of Himself. As we meet them He comes to us in larger fullness for each new necessity.

Lord, help me to see Thee in all my trying situations and to make them vessels to hold more of Thy grace.

Take no thought for your life
—Matthew 6:25.

The Lord is still using the things that are despised. The very names of Nazarene and Christian were once epithets of contempt. No man can have God's highest thought and be popular with his immediate generation. The most abused men are often the most used.

There are far greater calamities than to be unpopular and misunderstood. There are far worse things than to be found in the minority. Many of God's greatest blessings are lying behind the devil's scarecrows of prejudice and misrepresentation. The Holy Spirit is not ashamed to use unpopular people. And if He uses them, what need they care for men?

Oh, let us but have God's recognition and man's notice will count for little, and God will give us all we need of human help and praise. Let us only seek God's will, His glory, His approval. Let us go for Him on the hardest errands and do for Him the most menial tasks. It will be honor enough that He sends us and uses us. Let us not fear in this day to follow Him outside the camp, bearing His reproach. By-and-by he will own our worthless name before the myriads of earth and heaven.

*According to the power that worketh
in us—Ephesians 3:20.*

W hen we reach the place of union with God through the indwelling of the Holy Spirit, we come into the inheritance of external blessing and enter upon the land of our possession. Then our physical health and strength come to us through the power of our interior life. Then the prayer is fulfilled that we shall be in health and prosper as our soul prospers. Then, with the kingdom of God and His righteousness within us all things are added unto us.

God's external working always keeps pace with the power that works in us. When God is enthroned in a human soul, the devil and the world soon find it out. We do not need to advertise our power. Jesus could not be hid, and a soul filled with divine power and purity should become the center of attraction to hungry hearts and suffering lives.

Let us receive Him and recognize Him in His indwelling glory, and then will we appropriate all that it means for our life in all its fullness.

Lord, give me the "hiding of thy power," and let Christ be glorified in me.

To obey is better than sacrifice
—1 Samuel 15:22.

Our healing is represented as a special recompense for obedience. If, therefore, we would please the Lord and have the reward of those who please Him, there is no service so acceptable to Him as our praise.

Let us ever meet Him with a glad and thankful heart, and He will reflect it back in the radiance of our countenance and the buoyant life and springing health which are but the echo of a joyful heart.

Further, thankfulness is the best preparation for faith. Trust grows spontaneously in the praiseful heart. Thankfulness takes the sunny side of the street and looks at the bright side of God, and it is only thus that we can ever trust Him. Unbelief looks at our troubles and, of course, they seem like mountains, and faith is discouraged by the prospect. A thankful disposition will always find some cause for cheer, and a gloomy one will find a cloud in the brightest sky and a fly in the sweetest ointment. Let us cultivate a spirit of cheerfulness, and we shall find so much in God and in our lives to encourage us that we shall have no room for doubt or fear.

Happy are ye if ye do them—John 13:17.

You little know the rest that comes from the yielded will, the surrendered choice, the meek and lowly heart that lets the world go by and knows that it shall inherit the earth which it has refused. You little know the relish that it gives to the blessing to hunger and thirst after righteousness and to be filled with a satisfaction that worldly delight cannot afford. You little know what it is to then rise to the higher blessedness of the merciful, the forgiving, the hearts that have learned that it is "more blessed to give than to receive," and the lives that find that "letting go is twice possessing" and blessing others is to be doubly blessed.

There is yet one jewel brighter than all the rest in this crown of beatitudes. It is the teardrop crystallized into the diamond, the blood drop transfigured into the ruby of heaven's eternal crown. It is the joy of suffering with Jesus and then forgetting all the sorrow in the overflowing joy until with the heavenly Pascal we know not which to say first and so we say them both together, "Tears upon tears, joy upon joy."

Lead me in the way everlasting
—Psalm 139:24.

There is often apparently but little difference in two distinct lives between the person in constant victory and the one in frequent victory. But that little difference constitutes a world of success or failure. The one is the divine, the other is the human; the one is the everlasting way, the other the transient and the imperfect way. God wants to lead us to the way everlasting and to establish us and make us immovable as He.

We little know the seriousness of the slightest infraction of our surrender to God. It is but the first step in the downward progression, and only God knows where it shall end. Let us be *not of them who draw back unto perdition; but of them that believe to the saving of the soul* (Hebrews 10:39).

Our victory today is preparing the way for a greater victory tomorrow; but our small compromise today is opening the door for a more terrible defeat in the days to come. Let us, therefore, whatever we have claimed from our blessed Master, commit it to His keeping and take Him to establish us and hold us fast in the rejoicing of the hope firm unto the end.

Afterward that which is spiritual
—1 Corinthians 15:46.

God often has to bring us not only into the place of suffering, and the bed of sickness and pain, but also into the place where our righteousness breaks down and our character falls to pieces in order to humble us in the dust and show us the need of entire crucifixion to all our natural life. Then, at the feet of Jesus we are ready to receive Him, to abide in Him, depend upon Him alone and draw all our life and strength each moment from Him, our Living Head.

It was thus that Peter was saved by his very fall and had to die to Peter that he might live more perfectly to Christ. Have we thus died, and have we thus renounced the strength of our own self-confidence?

We begin life with the natural, next we come into the spiritual; but then, when we have truly received the kingdom of God and His righteousness, the natural is added to the spiritual, and we are able to receive the gifts of His providence and the blessings of life without becoming centered in them or allowing them to separate us from Him.

Who hath despised the day of small things?—Zechariah 4:10.

The oak comes out of the acorn, the eagle out of that little egg in the nest, the harvest out of the seed. Thus the glory of the coming age is coming out of the Christ-life now, even as the majesty of His kingdom was all wrapped up that night in the baby in Bethlehem.

Let us take Jesus for our total lives. Let us be united to His person and His risen body. Let us know what it is to say, *The body is . . . for the Lord; and the Lord is for the body* (1 Corinthians 6:13). *We are members of his body, of his flesh, and of his bones* (Ephesians 5:30).

He who gave that little infant, His only begotten Son, on that dark winter night to the arms of a cruel and ungrateful world will not refuse to give Him to us in all His fullness if we will but open our hearts and give Him right of way and full ownership and possession. Then we shall know in measure His quickening life, even as our hope shall reach its full fruition when we sit with Him on His throne with every fiber of our immortal beings even as He.

The God of Israel hath separated you
—Numbers 16:9.

The little plant may grow out of a pile of refuse and be surrounded by filth and covered with the dust that floats on the breeze, but its white roots are separated from the unclean soil, and its leaves and flowers have no affinity with the dust that settles upon them. After a shower of summer rain they throw off every particle of defilement and look up as fresh and spotless as before. Their intrinsic nature cannot have any part with these defiling things.

This is the separation which Christ requires and which He gives. There is no merit in my staying from the theater if I want to go. There is no value in my abstaining from the foolish novel or the intoxicating bottle if I am continually wishing I could have them. My heart is there, and my soul is defiled by the desire for evil things. It is not the world that stains us, but the love of the world. The true Levite is separated from the desire for earthly things, and even if he could, he would not have the forbidden pleasures which others prize.

··

Come ye yourselves apart—Mark 6:31.

One of the greatest hindrances to spirituality is the lack of waiting upon God. We cannot go through 24 hours with just the breaths of air we inhale as we sip our morning coffee. We must, rather, live in the atmosphere and breathe it all day long.

Christians do not wait upon God enough. It requires hours and hours daily of spiritual communion with the Holy Spirit to keep our vitality healthful and full. Every moment should find us breathing out ourselves into Christ, and breathing afresh His life.

God is waiting to send us the Holy Spirit. He is longing to bless us. His one business is to quicken and sustain our spiritual life with His infinite and great resources. Let us receive Him. Let us live in Him. Let us give to Him the joy of knowing that His infinite grace has not been bestowed in vain, but that we appreciate and appropriate the blessings He bestows.

Lord, help me this day to dwell in Thee as the flower in the sunshine, as the fish in the sea, living in Thy love as the atmosphere and element of my being.

He breathed on them—John 20:22.

The beautiful figure suggested by the words "He breathed on them" is full of simple instruction. It is as easy to receive the Holy Spirit as it is to breathe. It almost seems as if the Lord had given His disciples the very impression of breathing, and had said, "Now this is the way to receive the Holy Spirit."

It is not necessary for us to go to the isolation room of a hospital to have our lungs contaminated with impure air. All we need to do is to keep in our lungs the air we inhaled a minute ago, and it will kill us. All the pure elements have been absorbed from it, and there is nothing left but carbon and other deadly gases.

Therefore, if we are to be filled with the Holy Spirit, we must first be emptied not only of our old sinful life, but of our old spiritual life. We must take a new breath every moment, or we will die. God wants us to empty out all our being into Him. Then we can take Him in— without needing to try too hard.

A vacuum always becomes filled; an empty pair of lungs unavoidably breathes in the pure air. If we are only in the right attitude, there will be no trouble about receiving the Holy Spirit.

Finally, my brethren, rejoice in the Lord—Philippians 3:1.

There is no spiritual value in depression. One bright and thankful look at the cross is worth a thousand morbid, self-condemning reflections. The longer you look at the evil the more it defiles and mesmerizes you into its own likeness. Lay it down at the cross, accept the cleansing blood, reckon yourself dead to the thing that was wrong, then rise up and count yourself as if you were another man or woman.

Identifying yourself with the Lord Jesus, you may then accept your standing in Him and look in your Father's face as blameless as Jesus. Then out of your every fault will come some lesson of watchfulness or some secret of victory that will enable you some day to thank Him, even for your painful experiences.

But praise is a sacrifice for it is acceptable to God. It ascends to heaven sweeter than the songs of angels, *a sweetsmelling savour* (Ephesians 5:2) to your Lord. It should be *the sacrifice of praise to God continually* (Hebrews 13:15). One drop of poison will make the whole cup a cup of death, and one moment of gloom will defile a whole day of sunshine. Let us *rejoice evermore* (1 Thessalonians 5:16).

I will joy in the God of my salvation
—Habakkuk 3:18.

The secret of joy is not to wait until you *feel* happy, but to rise, by an act of faith, out of the depression which is dragging you down and begin to praise God as an act of choice. This is the meaning of such passages as these: *Rejoice in the Lord alway: and again I say, Rejoice* (Philippians 4:4). *I therein do rejoice, yea, and will rejoice* (Philippians 1:18). *Count it all joy when ye fall into divers temptations* (James 1:2). In all these cases there is an evident struggle with sadness and then the triumphs of faith and praise.

This is what is meant—at least in part—by the sacrifice of praise. A sacrifice is that which costs us something. And when a man or woman has some cherished grudge or wrong and is harboring it, nursing it, dwelling on it, and quite determined to enjoy a miserable time in selfish grumbling, it costs us no little sacrifice to throw off the morbid spell, to rise out of the mood of self-commiseration in wholesome and holy determination and say, *I will rejoice in the Lord* (Habakkuk 3:18); *I will count it all joy* (James 1:2).

He that eateth me, even he shall live
by me—John 6:57.

What the children of God need is not merely a lot of teaching, but the Living Bread. The best wheat is not good food. It must be ground and baked before it can be digested and assimilated to nourish the system. The purest and the highest truth cannot of itself sanctify or satisfy a living soul.

Christ breathes the New Testament message from His mouth with a breath of quickening power. It is as we abide in Him, and drink in His very life that we are nourished, quickened, comforted and healed.

This is the secret of divine healing. It is not believing a doctrine, it is not performing a ceremony, it is not wringing a petition from the heavens by the logic of faith and the force of our wills; it is the inbreathing of the life of God, it is the living touch which none can understand except those whose senses are exercised to know the realities of the unseen world. Often, therefore, a very little truth will bring us much more help and blessing than a great amount of instruction.

All things are lawful for me
—1 Corinthians 10:23.

I may be perfectly free myself to do many things, the doing of which might hurt my brother and wound his conscience. Love will gladly surrender the little indulgence so that my brother may be saved from temptation. There are many questions which are easily settled by this principle.

So, too, there are many forms of recreation which in themselves might be harmless and, under certain circumstances, unobjectionable, but they have become associated with worldliness and godlessness and have proved snares and temptations to many a younger Christian. In that case, the law of love would lead me to avoid them, discountenance them and in no way give encouragement to others to participate in them.

It is just in these things that are not required of us by absolute rules, but are the impulses of a thoughtful love, that the highest qualities of Christian character show themselves. It is in these that the most delicate shades of Christian love are manifested.

Wherefore receive ye one another, as Christ also received us to the glory of God—Romans 15:7.

Our text sets forth a sublime principle, and it will give sublimity to all of life. It is stated elsewhere in similar language, *Whatsoever ye do in word or deed, do all in the name of the Lord Jesus* (Colossians 3:17).

This is our high calling, to represent Christ and act in His behalf and in His character and spirit under all circumstances and toward all persons. "What would Jesus do?" is a simple question which will settle every difficulty, and always settle it on the side of love.

But we cannot answer this question rightly without having Jesus Himself in our hearts. We cannot *act* Christ. This is too grave a matter for acting. We must *have* Christ and simply be natural and true to the life within us. Then that life within us will act itself out.

How easy it is to love everyone and see nothing but loveliness, when our hearts are filled with Christ. How every difficulty melts away and everyone we meet seems clothed with the Spirit within us when we are filled with His presence.

Lo, I am with you alway, even unto the end of the world—Matthew 28:20.

Literally, Jesus is saying, "I am with you all the days." He comes to us each day with a new blessing. Every morning, day by day, He walks with us with a love that never tires and a blessing that never grows old. And He is with us "all the days"; it is a ceaseless abiding. There is no day so dark, so commonplace, so uninteresting that we do not find Him there.

Often, no doubt, He is unrecognized, as He was on the way to Emmaus, until we realize how our hearts have been warmed, our love stirred, our Bible so strangely vivified, with every promise seeming to speak to us with heavenly reality and power. It is the Lord!

God grant that His living presence may be made more real to us henceforth. Whether we have the consciousness and evidence—as they had a few glorious times in those 40 days—or whether we go forth into the coming days as they did most of their days to walk by simple faith and in simple duty, let us know this fact always, that He is with us, a Presence all unseen but real and ready when we need Him to manifest Himself for our relief.

The furnace for gold; but the Lord trieth the hearts—Proverbs 17:3.

Remember that temptation is not sin unless it is accompanied with the consent of your will. There may seem to be even the inclination, and yet the real choice of your spirit is fixed immovably against it, and God regards it simply as a solicitation and credits you with an obedience all the more pleasing to Him because the temptation was so strong.

We little know how evil can find access to a pure nature and seem to incorporate itself with our thoughts and feelings. When, however, we resist and overcome it we remain as pure as the sea fowl that emerges from the water without a single drop remaining upon its burnished wing. The harp, struck by a rude or clumsy hand, gives forth a discordant sound—not from any defect of the instrument, but because of the hand that touches it. But when the Master's hand plucks the strings it produces chords of exquisite delight.

In nothing terrified by your adversaries: which is to them an evident token of perdition, but to you of salvation, and that of God (Philippians 1:28).

*Think it not strange concerning the fiery
trial which is to try you—1 Peter 4:12.*

Most persons after a step of faith are looking
for sunny skies and unruffled seas, and
when they meet a storm and tempest they are
filled with astonishment and perplexity. But this
is just what we must expect to meet if we have
received anything of the Lord. The best token of
His presence is the adversary's defiance. The
more real our blessing, the more certainly it will
be challenged. It is a good thing to go out looking
for the worst, and if it comes we are not surprised. To the contrary, if our path is smooth and
our way unopposed, it is all the more delightful
because it comes unexpectedly.

But let us quite understand what we mean by
temptation. It you have stepped out with the
assurance that you have died to self and sin, you
may be greatly amazed to find yourself assailed
with a tempest of thoughts and feelings that seem
to come wholly from within, and you will be impelled to say, "Why, I thought I was dead, but I
seem to be alive." This, beloved, is the time to
remember that temptation itself is not sin, it is a
tactic of the evil one.

*For the Lord God will help me; therefore
shall I not be confounded: therefore
have I set my face like a flint, and I
know that I shall not be ashamed*
—Isaiah 50:7.

Here is the language of trust and victory. It was through this faith, as we are told in Hebrews, that in His last agony Jesus *for the joy that was set before him endured the cross, despising the shame* (12:2). His life was a life of faith, His death was a victory of faith, His resurrection was a triumph of faith, His mediatorial reign is one long victory of faith, *from henceforth expecting till his enemies be made his footstool* (10:13).

And so, for us He has become the pattern of faith. In every situation of difficulty, temptation and distress He has gone before us, waving the banner of trust and triumph and bidding us to follow in His victorious footsteps.

He is the great Pattern Believer. While we must claim our salvation by faith, the great Forerunner also claimed the world's salvation by the same faith.

Let us therefore consider this glorious Leader our perfect example, and as we follow close behind Him, let us remember that where He has triumphed we may triumph, too.

Though it tarry, wait for it; for it will surely come, and will not tarry
—Habakkuk 2:3.

Some things have their cycle in an hour and some in a century. Long or short, God's plans shall complete their cycle. The tender annual which blossoms for a season and dies, and the American aloe which develops in a century—each is true to its normal principle. Many of us desire to pluck our fruit in June rather than wait until October, and so, of course, the fruit is sour and immature. But God's purposes ripen slowly and fully, and faith waits while it tarries knowing it will surely come and will not tarry too long.

It is perfect rest to fully learn and wholly trust this glorious promise. We may know without a question that His purposes shall be accomplished when we have fully committed our ways to Him and are walking in watchful obedience to His every prompting. This faith will give a calm and tranquil poise to the spirit and save us from restless fretting and trying to do too much ourselves.

> Wait, and every wrong will righten,
> Wait, and every cloud will brighten,
> If you only wait.

I will never leave thee, nor forsake thee—Hebrews 13:5.

It is most cheering to know that although we err and bring upon ourselves many troubles that might easily have been averted, yet God does not forsake even His mistaken child, but on his humble repentance and supplication is ever ready both to pardon and deliver.

Let us not give up our faith because we have perhaps stepped out of the path in which He would have led us. The Israelites did not follow when He called them into the Land of Promise, yet God did not desert them. During the forty years of their wandering He walked by their side, bearing their backsliding with patient compassion, waiting to be gracious to them when another generation came. *In all their affliction he was afflicted, and the angel of his presence saved them; . . . he bare them, and carried them all the days of old* (Isaiah 63:9). So it is today, while our wanderings bring us many sorrows and lose us many blessings, to the heart that truly chooses His, He has graciously said: *I will never leave thee, nor forsake thee.*

....

The people shall be [a freewill offering] in the day of thy power
—Psalm 110:3.

This is what the term consecration properly means. It is the voluntary or self-offering of the heart, by the constraint of love, to be the Lord's. Its glad expression is, *I am my beloved's* (Song of Solomon 6:3).

Surrender must spring, of course, from faith. There must be the full confidence that we are safe in this abandonment, that we are not falling over a precipice or surrendering ourselves to the hands of a judge but we are sinking into a Father's arms and stepping into an infinite inheritance. And it *is* an infinite inheritance!

It is an infinite privilege to be permitted to relinquish ourselves to One who pledges Himself to make us all that we would love to be, yes, all that His infinite wisdom, power and love will delight to accomplish in us. It is the clay yielding itself to the potter's hands that it may be shaped into a vessel of honor meet for the Master's use. It is the poor street waif consenting to become the child of a prince in order that he may be educated, provided for and prepared to inherit all the wealth of his guardian.

We walk by faith, not by sight
—2 Corinthians 5:7.

There are heavenly notes which have power to break down adamant walls and dissolve difficult mountains. The song of Paul and Silas burst the fetters of the Philippian jail; the choir of Jehoshaphat put to flight the armies of the Ammonites. Even so the song of faith will disperse our adversaries and lift our sinking hearts into strength and victory.

Is this a dark hour in your life? Is it the winter of barrenness and gloom? Remember that it is God's chosen time for the education of faith, and that He conceals beneath the surface precious and untold harvests of unthought-of fruit! It will not always be night. And when the morning comes and spring spreads its verdant mantle over the barren fields, then we shall be glad that we did not disappoint our Father in the hour of testing, but our faith had already claimed and seen in the distance the glad fruition which sight now beholds.

Lord, help me to believe when I cannot see and to learn from my trials to trust Thee more.

In due season we shall reap, if we faint not—Galatians 6:9.

If the least of us could only anticipate the eternal issues that will probably spring from the humblest services of faith, we would count our sacrifices and labors occasions of honor and opportunity and would cease to speak of trials and sacrifices for God.

The smallest grain of faith is a deathless and incorruptible germ which will yet plant the heavens and cover the earth with harvests of imperishable glory. Let us lift up our heads, for the horizon is wider than the little circle that we can see. We are living, we are suffering, we are laboring, we are trusting for the ages yet to come. *Let us not be weary in well doing: for in due season we shall reap, if we faint not.* With tears of pure rapture we shall cry some day, *Oh how great is thy goodness, which thou hast laid up for them that fear thee; which thou hast wrought for them that trust in thee before the sons of men!* (Psalm 31:19).

Lord, help me today to live under the powers of the world to come and to live as one in heaven yet walking upon the earth.

....

They shall not be ashamed that wait
—Isaiah 49:23.

Often God calls us aside from our work for a season and bids us be still and learn before we begin again to minister. Especially is this so when there has been some serious break, some sudden failure or some radical defect in our work. There is no time lost in such waiting hours.

Fleeing from his enemies, the ancient knight found that his horse needed to be reshod. Prudence seemed to urge him on, but higher wisdom taught him to halt a few minutes at the blacksmith's forge to have the shoe replaced. Though he heard the feet of his pursuers galloping hard behind, yet he waited those minutes until his charger was refitted for his flight. Then, leaping into his saddle just as they appeared a hundred yards away, he dashed away from them with the fleetness on the wind. He knew that his halting had hastened his escape.

So often God bids us tarry and fully recover ourselves for the next great stage of our journey and work.

Lord, teach me to be still and know that Thou art God, and all this day to walk with Thee.

Faint, yet pursuing—Judges 8:4.

It is a good thing to learn to depend upon God to work through our feeble resources and yet, while so depending, to be absolutely faithful and diligent and not allow our trust to deteriorate into indolence.

We find no sloth or negligence in Gideon or his three hundred; though they were weak and few, they were completely loyal, and everything in them—down to their last breath—was ready for God to use. *Faint, yet pursuing* was their watchword as they followed and finished their glorious victory. They did not rest until the last of their enemies was destroyed, and even their false friends were punished for their treachery and unfaithfulness.

God still calls the weakest instruments. When, however, he chooses and enables them, they are no longer weak but *mighty through God* (2 Corinthians 10:4) and faithful through His grace to every trust and opportunity. "They trust," as Dr. Chalmers used to say, "as though all depended upon God, and work as though all depended upon themselves."

Teach me, my blessed Master, to trust and obey.

We see not yet all things put under him.
But we see Jesus—Hebrews 2:8-9.

How true is our text for us all! How many things there are that seem to be stronger than we are, but blessed be Jesus' name they are all in subjection under Him, and we see Him crowned above them all.

Jesus is our Head, our representative, our other self, and where He is we shall surely be. Therefore when we fail to see something that God has promised, and that we have claimed in our experience, let us look up and see it realized in Him and claim it in Him. Our side is only half the circle; the heavenly side is already complete. The rainbow, the upper half of which we cannot see, shall one day be all around the throne and include the other hemisphere of all our now unfinished life.

By faith, then, let us enter into all our inheritance. Let us lift up our eyes to the north, south, east and west, and hear Him say, *All the land that thou seest, to thee will I give it* (Genesis 13:15). Let us remember that the circle is complete, that the inheritance is unlimited and that all things are put under His feet.

I am the Lord that healeth thee
—Exodus 15:26.

It is very reasonable that God should expect us to trust Him for our bodies as well as our souls. If our faith is not practical enough to bring us temporal relief, how can we be schooled to depend upon God for anything that involves serious risk?

It is all very well to talk about trusting God for the distant and future prospect of salvation after death. There is scarcely a sinner in a Christian land who does not trust to be saved some day, but there is no grasp in faith like this. It is only when we come face to face with positive issues and overwhelming forces that we can prove the reality of divine power in a supernatural life. As an education to our spirits as well as a gracious provision for our temporal bodies, God has always trained His people to recognize Him as the supply of all their needs, and to look to Him as the Physician of their bodies and the Father of their spirits. Have we learned the meaning of Jehovah-rophi? (see Exodus 15:23-27). Has it changed our Marah of trial into an Elim of blessing and praise?

God . . . calleth those things which be
not as though they were—Romans 4:17.

The Word of God creates what it commands. When Christ says to any of us *Now are ye clean through the word which I have spoken unto you* (John 15:3), we are clean. When He says *no condemnation* (Romans 8:1) there is none, though there may have been a lifetime of sin before. And when He says, *mighty through God to the pulling down of strong holds* (2 Corinthians 10:4), then the weak are strong. This is faith's part—to make it real.

A French commander thanked a common soldier who had saved his life and called him captain. Although he was only a private, the man took the commander at his word, accepted the new name and was thereby constituted indeed a captain.

Why not take God's creating words of justification, sanctification, power and deliverance and thus make real the mighty promise, *He giveth power to the faint; and to them that have no might he increaseth strength. . . . But they that wait upon the Lord shall renew their strength* (Isaiah 40:29, 31).

The faith of the Son of God
—Galatians 2:20.

L et us learn the secret of our faith. It is the faith of Christ, springing in our hearts and trusting in our trials. So shall we always sing, *The life which I now live in the flesh I live by the faith of the Son of God, who loved me, and gave himself for me* (Galatians 2:20). If we keep looking unto Jesus, *the author and finisher of our faith* (Hebrews 12:2), we shall discover that instead of struggling to appropriate the promises of God, we shall lie down upon them in blessed repose, and be borne up by them with the faith which is no more our own than the promises upon which it rests. Each new need will find us leaning again on Him for the grace to trust and to overcome.

Further, we see here the true spirit of prayer. It is the Spirit of Christ in us. *In the midst of the congregation will I praise thee* (Psalm 22:22). Christ still sings these praises in the trusting heart and lifts our prayers into songs of victory! This is the true spirit of prayer.

Paul and Silas in the prison at Philippi turned prayer into praise, night into day—the night of sorrow into the morning of joy. When Jesus, the spirit of faith is in us, He will also become the spirit of praise.

I will be with him in trouble
—Psalm 91:15.

We often ask the question, "Why didn't God help me sooner?" It is not His order. He must first adjust us to the situation and cause us to learn our lesson from it. His promise is, *I will be with him in trouble; I will deliver him, and honour him.* He first must be with us in the trouble until we grow quiet. Then He will take us out of it. This will not come until we have stopped being restless and fretful about it and have become calm and trustful. Then He will say, "It is enough."

God uses trouble to teach His children precious lessons. They are intended to educate us. When their good work is done, a glorious recompense will come to us through them. He does not regard them as difficulties but as opportunities. They have come to give God a greater interest in us and to show how he can deliver us from them. Without difficulties we cannot have a mercy worth praising God for. God is as deep, and long, and high as our little world of circumstances.

....

The glorious liberty of the children
of God—Romans 8:21.

Are you above self and self-pleasing in every way? Have you risen above circumstances so that you are not influenced by them? Are you above sickness and the evil forces around that would drag down your physical life into the quicksands? These forces are all around and if yielded to would quickly swamp us. God does not destroy sickness or its power to hurt, but He lifts us above it.

Are you above your feelings, moods, emotions and states? Can you sail immovable as the stars through all sorts of weather?

A harp will give out sweet music or discordant sounds as different fingers touch the strings. If the devil's hand is on your harp strings what hideous sounds they will produce. But let the fingers of the Lord sweep over them, and they will breathe out celestial music.

Are you lifted above people, so that you are not bound by or to anyone except in the Lord? Are you standing free in His glorious life?

> I am risen with Christ,
>   I am dwelling above;
> I am walking with Jesus below,
> I am shedding the light of His glory
>   and love
> Around me wherever I go.

The trial of your faith, being much more precious than gold—1 Peter 1:7.

Our trials are great opportunities. Too often we look on them as great obstacles. It would be a heaven of rest if each of us would recognize every difficult situation as one of God's chosen ways of proving to us His love and power. It would be an inspiration of unspeakable power if, instead of calculating upon defeat, we should begin to look around for the messages of His glorious manifestations. Then indeed every cloud would become a rainbow and every mountain a path of ascension and a scene of tranfiguration.

If we will look upon the past, many of us will find that the very time our heavenly Father has chosen to do the kindest things for us and give us the richest blessings has been the time when we were under great pressure and hemmed in on every side. God's jewels are often sent to us in rough packages, but within we find the very treasures of the King's palace and the Bridegroom's love.

> Fire of God, thy work begin,
> Burn up the dross of self and sin;
> Burn off my fetters, set me free,
> And through the furnace walk with me.

Call not thou common—Acts 10:15.
There is nothing unclean of itself
—Romans 14:14.

We can bring Christ into common things as fully as into what we call religious services. It would seem that the highest and hardest application of divine grace is to bring it down to the ordinary matters of life. God is, therefore, far more honored in this than even in things that are more especially sacred.

In Romans 12, which is the manual of practical consecration, just after the apostle speaks of ministering in sacred things, he begins to discuss the common, social and secular affairs into which we are to bring our consecration principles. We read: *Be kindly affectioned one to another with brotherly love; in honor preferring one another; not slothful in business; fervent in spirit; serving the Lord* (vv. 10-11).

God wanted the Levites scattered all over the cities of Israel. He wants our workshops, factories, kitchens, nurseries, editors' rooms and printing offices as much as our pulpits and prayer closets. He wants us to be just as holy at high noon on Monday or Wednesday as in the sanctuary on Sunday morning.

O my dove, that art in the clefts
of the rock, in the secret places of
the stairs—Song of Solomon 2:14.

The dove is in the cleft of the rock—the riven side of our Lord. There is comfort and security there. It is also in the secret places of the stairs. It loves to build its nest in the high towers to which men mount by winding stairs for hundreds of feet above the ground. What a glorious vision is there obtained of the surrounding scenery. It is a picture of ascending life.

To reach our highest altitudes we must find the secret places of the stairs. That is the only way to rise above the natural plane. Our lives should be ones of quiet mounting with occasional resting places; but we should be mounting higher, step by step. Not everyone finds this way of secret ascent. It is only for God's chosen. The world may think we are going down. We may not have as much public work to do as formerly. *Blessed are the poor in spirit* (Matthew 5:3). It is a secret, hidden life. We may be hardly aware that we are growing, until one day a test comes and we find we are established.

Have you arrived at the place where Christ is keeping you from willful disobedience? Does the consciousness of sin make you shudder? Are you lifted above the world?

*That in the ages to come he might
show the exceeding riches of his grace
—Ephesians 2:7.*

Christ's great purpose for His people is to
train them to know *the hope of [their] calling,
and . . . the riches of the glory of their inheritance, . . . and
what . . . the exceeding greatness of his power to usward
who believe* (Ephesians 1:18-19).

Let us prove, in all our varied walks of life and
scenes of conflict, the fullness of His power and
grace, and thus shall we know *in the ages to come
. . . the exceeding riches of his grace in his kindness
toward us through Christ Jesus.*

Are we thus following our Teacher in the
school of faith, and finishing the education which
is to fit us for *a far more exceeding and eternal weight
of glory?* (2 Corinthians 4:17).

Little can we now dream what these lessons
will mean for us some day when we sit with Him
on His throne and share with Him the power of
God and the government of the universe. Let us
be faithful students now, and soon with Him we,
too, will have *endured the cross, despising the shame,*
and shall sit down *at the right hand of the throne of
God* (Hebrews 12:2).

Moses gave not any inheritance: the
Lord God of Israel was their inheritance,
as he said unto them—Joshua 13:33.

The procedure was very significant. God gave the land to the other tribes of Israel, but He gave Himself to the Levites. There is such a thing in the Christian life as an inheritance from the Lord, and there is such a thing as having the Lord Himself for our inheritance.

Some people receive a sanctification from the Lord that is of much value, but variable and often impermanent. Others have learned the higher lesson of taking the Lord Himself to be their keeper and their sanctity, and abiding in Him they are kept above the vicissitudes of their own states and feelings.

Some receive from the Lord large measures of joy and blessing and times of refreshing. Others, again, learn to take the Lord Himself as their joy.

Some people are content to have peace with God, but others have taken *the peace of God, which passeth all understanding* (Philippians 4:7).

Some have faith *in* God, while others have the faith *of* God. Some have many touches of healing from God, others have learned to live in the very health of God Himself.

The little foxes, that spoil the vines
—Song of Solomon 2:15.

There are some things good without being perfect. You do not need to have a whole regiment firing outside your room to wake you. It is quite enough that your alarm clock rings. It is not necessary to fret about everything; it is quite enough if the devil gets your mind rasped with one little worry, one little thought which destroys your perfect peace.

It is like the polish on an exquisite table top. One scratch will destroy it; and the finer it is, the smaller the scratch that will deface it. And so your rest can be destroyed by a very little thing. Perhaps you have trusted in God about your future salvation; have you trusted Him about your present business or earthly cares, your money and your family?

What is meant by the *peace [that] passeth all understanding?* (Philippians 4:7). It does not mean a peace no one can comprehend. It means a peace no amount of reasoning will bring. You cannot get it by thinking. There may be perfect bewilderment and perplexity all around the horizon, yet your heart can rest in perfect security because God knows, He loves, He leads.

Instead of the brier shall come up the myrtle tree—Isaiah 55:13.

God's sweetest memorial is the transformed thorn and thistle blooming with flowers of peace and goodness where once recriminations grew.

God is waiting to make just such memorials in your life out of the things that are hurting you most today. Take the grievances, the separations, the strained friendships and the broken ties which have been the sorrow and heartbreak of your life and let God heal them. Allow Him to give you grace that can make you right with all those with whom you have been wrong. You will wonder at the joy and blessing that will come out of the things that have caused you nothing but regret and pain.

Blessed are the peacemakers: for they shall be called the children of God (Matthew 5:9). The everlasting employment of our blessed Redeemer is to reconcile the guilty and the estranged from God. The highest and most Christlike work that we can do is to be like Him.

Shall we go forth to dry the tears of a sorrowing world, to heal the brokenhearted, to bind up the wounds of human lives, and to unite heart to heart and earth to heaven?

He that triumphed gloriously
—Exodus 15:1.

God calls us to victory. Have you given up the conflict, have you surrendered? Have you said, "This thing is too much"? Have you said, "I can give up anything else but this"?

If you have, you are not in the land of promise. God intends that you accept every difficult thing that comes into your life. He has started with you, knowing every difficulty, and if you dare to let Him, He will carry you through not only to be a conqueror but "more than conquerors."

Are you looking for all the victory God has for you? God gives His children strength for the battle and watches over them with a fond enthusiasm. He longs to fold you close and say to you, "I have seen thy conflict, I have watched thy trials, I have rejoiced in thy victory; thou hast honored Me." Remember what he told Joshua at the begining, *There shall not any man be able to stand before thee all the days of thy life: as I was with Moses, so will I be with thee: I will not fail thee, nor forsake thee* (Joshua 1:5). And again, His word to us is, *Fear . . . not, for I am with thee* (Isaiah 41:10).

Ephraim, he hath mixed himself
—Hosea 7:8.

It is a great thing to learn to take God first. Then He can afford to give us everything else without the fear of its hurting us.

As long as you want anything very much, especially more than you want God, it is an idol. When you become satisfied with God, however, everything else so loses its charm that He can give it to you without harm. Then you can take just as much as you choose and use it for His glory.

There is no harm whatever in having money, houses, lands, friends and children if you do not value these things or ones for themselves.

If you have been separated from them in spirit and become satisfied with God Himself, then they will become to you channels to be filled with God and to bring Him nearer to you. Then every little lamb around your household will be a tender cord to bind you to the Shepherd's heart. Then every affection will be a golden cup filled with the wine of His love. Then every bank, stock and investment will be but a channel through which you can pour out His benevolence and extend His grace.

He opened not his mouth—Isaiah 53:7.

How much grace it requires to bear a misunderstanding rightly and to receive an unkind judgment in holy sweetness! Nothing tests the Christian character more than to have some evil thing said about us. This is the file that soon proves whether we are electroplate or solid gold. If we could only know the blessings that lie hidden in our lives, we would say like David, when Shimei cursed him, *Let him curse; . . . It may be the Lord will . . . requite me good for his cursing this day* (2 Samuel 16:11-12).

Some people get easily turned aside from the grandeur of their life work by pursuing their own grievances and enemies. Soon their lives become one little whirl of petty warfare. It is like a nest of hornets. We may disperse the hornets, but we will probably get terribly stung and get nothing for our pains, for even their honey is not worth a search.

God give us more of Jesus' Spirit. *When he was reviled, [he] reviled not again; . . . but committed himself to him that judgeth righteously* (1 Peter 2:23).

Consider him that endured such contradiction of sinners against himself (Hebrews 12:3).

*There failed not ought of any good thing
which the Lord had spoken
—Joshua 21:45.*

Some day even you, trembling faltering one,
shall stand upon those heights that Joshua
knew. As you look back upon all you have passed
through, all you have narrowly escaped, all the
perils through which He guided you, the stumblings through which He guarded you and the
sins from which He saved you; you will shout,
with a meaning you cannot understand now,
*Salvation to our God, which sitteth upon the throne,
and unto the Lamb* (Revelation 7:10).

Some day He will sit down with us in that glorious home, and we shall have all the ages in
which to understand the story of our lives. He
will read over again this marked old Bible with
us, He will show us how He kept all these
promises, He will explain to us the mysteries
that we could not understand, He will recall all
the finished story. Then I am sure we will cry:
"Blessed Christ! you have been so true, you have
been so good! Was there ever love like this?"
And then the great chorus will be repeated once
more—*There failed not ought of any good thing which
the Lord had spoken; . . . all came to pass.*

....

Peace be unto you—John 20:21.

Peace be unto you. These words are a type of Jesus' first appearing to our hearts when He comes to bring us His peace and to teach us to trust Him and to love Him.

But there is a second peace which He has to give. Jesus said unto them again, *Peace be unto you.* There is a "peace," and there is an "again peace." There is a peace *with* God, and there is *the peace of God, which passeth all understanding* (Philippians 4:7). It is the deeper peace that we need before we can serve Him or be used for His glory.

While we are burdened with our own cares, He cannot give us His. While we are occupied with ourselves, we cannot be at leisure to serve Him. Our minds will be so filled with our own anxieties that we would not be equal to the trust which He requires of us. Before He can entrust us with His work, He wants to deliver us from every burden and anxiety.

> Peace, perfect peace, in this
>   dark world of sin?
> The blood of Jesus whispers
>   peace within.
> Peace, perfect peace, by thronging
>   duties pressed?
> To do the will of Jesus, this is rest.

*If ye through the Spirit do mortify
the deeds of the body, ye shall
live—Romans 8:13.*

The Holy Spirit is the only one who can kill us and keep us dead. Many Christians try to do this disagreeable work themselves, and they are going through a continual crucifixion but can never accomplish the work permanently. This is the work of the Holy Spirit, and when we really yield ourselves to the death, it is delightful to find how sweetly He can execute the sentence.

They tell us that by the touch of the electric spark life is extinguished almost without a quiver of pain. However this may be in natural things, we know the Holy Spirit can touch with celestial fire the surrendered thing, after it is really yielded up to the sentence of death, and slay it in a moment. The yielding is our business, and it is God's business to execute the sentence and to keep it constantly operative.

May we not live in the pain of perpetual and ineffective suicide, but reckoning ourselves dead indeed, let us leave ourselves in the hands of the blessed Holy Spirit. He will slay whatever rises in opposition to His will and keep us true to our heavenly reckoning and filled with His resurrection life.

And he that searcheth the hearts
knoweth what is the mind of the Spirit,
because he maketh intercession for the
saints according to the will of God
—Romans 8:2.

The Holy Spirit becomes to the consecrated heart the Spirit of intercession. We have two Advocates. We have an Advocate with the Father, who prays for us at God's right hand. We also have the Holy Spirit, the Advocate within who prays in us, inspiring our petitions and presenting them, through Christ, to God.

We need this Advocate. We know not what to pray for and we know not how to pray as we ought, but He breathes in the holy heart the desires that we may not always understand, the groanings which we could not utter.

God understands, and He, with a loving Father's heart, is always searching our hearts to find the Spirit's prayer and to answer it. He finds many a prayer there that we have not discovered, and answers many a cry that we never understood. And when we reach our heavenly home and read the records of life, we shall better know and appreciate the infinite love of that Divine Friend who has watched within as the Spirit of prayer and breathed out our every need to the heart of God.

The law of the Spirit of life in Christ
Jesus hath made me free—Romans 8:2.

The life of Jesus Christ brought into our hearts by the Holy Spirit operates there as a new law of divine strength and vitality. It counteracts, overcomes and lifts us above the old law of sin and death.

Let us illustrate these two laws by a simple comparison. By the law of gravity my hand naturally falls upon the desk and lies there, attracted downward by that natural law which makes heavy bodies fall to the earth.

But there is a stronger law than the law of gravity—my own life and will. Through the operation of this higher law—the law of vitality—I can defy the law of gravity, lift my hand and hold it above its former resting place and move it at my will. The law of vitality has freed me from the law of gravity.

Precisely so the indwelling life of Christ Jesus, operating with the power of a new law, lifts me above and counteracts the power of sin in my fallen nature.

*The carnal mind is enmity against
God—Romans 8:7.*

The flesh is incurably bad. *It is not subject to the
law of God, neither indeed can be.* It can never
be any better. It is no use trying to improve the
flesh. We may educate it all we please. We may
train it by the most approved methods, we may
set before it the brightest examples, we may pipe
to it or mourn before it, we may treat it with
encouragement or severity. But its nature will
always be incorrigibly the same.

The wild hawk which the little child captures
in its infancy and tries to train in the habits of
the dove will fasten its cruel beak upon the
gentle fingers that caress it, showing the old wild
spirit of fear and ferocity. So the flesh is a hawk
by nature, and it can never be made a dove. For
*the carnal mind is enmity against God: for it is not
subject to the law of God, neither indeed can be.*

The only remedy for human nature is to
destroy it and receive instead the divine nature.
God does not improve man. He crucifies the
natural life with Christ and creates the new man
in Christ Jesus.

··

Get thee behind me, Satan
—Matthew 16:23.

If when it seems your old self has come back, you listen to it, fear it, believe it, it will have the same influence upon you as if it were not dead. It will control you and destroy you. Instead, simply ignore it and say: "You are not I, you are Satan trying to make me believe that my old self is not dead. I refuse you. I treat you as a demon power outside of me, I detach myself from you." The evil thing will disappear, the shadow will vanish, the wand of faith will dispel the troubling spirit and send it back to the abyss. In its place we will find Christ there instead with His risen life to back up our confidence and seal our victory.

Satan can stand anything better than neglect. If we ignore him he becomes disgusted and disappears. Jesus turned His back upon him and said, *Get thee behind me, Satan.* So let us refuse him, and we shall find that he will be compelled to act according to our faith.

> Once I believed I must always
> be stumbling
> For my old nature was poisoned
> with sin;
> Now there's a mightier Power
> upholds me,
> Cleansing and keeping and
> dwelling within.

Faith is . . . the evidence of things not seen—Hebrews 11:1.

True faith drops its letter in the post office box and lets it go. Distrust holds onto a corner of it and wonders why the answer never comes.

In my desk are some letters that I wrote weeks ago. But there was some slight uncertainty about the address or the contents so they are yet unmailed. As yet they have not done me or anyone else any good. They will never accomplish anything until I let them go out of my hands and trust them to the postal system.

This is the case with true faith. It hands its case over to God and then He works.

There is an appropriate verse in Psalm 37: *Commit thy way unto the Lord; trust also in him; and he [worketh]* (v. 5). But He never works until we commit.

Faith is a receiving—or still better—a taking of God's proffered gifts. We may believe and come and commit and rest, but we will not fully realize all our blessing until we begin to receive and come into the attitude of abiding and taking.

Whereas thou hast been forsaken and hated, . . . I will make thee . . . a joy—Isaiah 60:15.

God loves to take the worst of lost men and make them the most magnificent memorials of His redeeming love and power. He loves to take the victims of Satan's hate and the most fearful examples of his power to destroy and use them to illustrate and illuminate the possibilities of divine mercy and the creativity of the Holy Spirit.

He loves to take the things in our own lives that have been the worst, the hardest and the most hostile to God, and to transform them so that we shall be the opposites of our former selves.

The sweetest spirits are made from the most stormy and self-willed; the mightiest faith is created out of the wilderness of doubts and fears; the divinest love is transformed out of stony hearts of hate and selfishness.

The grace of God is equal to the most uncongenial temperaments and to the most unfavorable circumstances. Its glory is to transform a curse into blessing and show to men and angels of ages yet to come that *where sin abounded, grace did much more abound* (Romans 5:20).

Abraham believed God—Romans 4:3.

Abraham's faith reposed in God Himself. He knew the God he was dealing with. It was a personal confidence in One whom he could utterly trust.

The real secret of Abraham's whole life was in his friendship with God. He knew God to be his great, good and faithful Friend. Taking Him at His word, he stepped out from all that he knew and loved and went forth upon an unknown pathway with none but God.

In addition to trusting in the Word of God, have we learned to lean our whole weight upon God, the God of infinite love and power, our covenant God and everlasting Friend?

We are told that Abraham glorified God by this life of faith. The truest way to glorify God is to let the world see what He is and what He can do. God does not so much want us to do things as to let people see what He can do. God is not looking for extraordinary characters as His instruments, but He is looking for humble instruments through whom He can be honored throughout the ages.

All things are naked and opened unto the eyes of him with whom we have to do —Hebrews 4:13.

The literal translation of that phrase in Hebrews is, "all things are stripped and stunned." Such is the force of the Greek words. The figure is that of an athlete in the Coliseum who has fought his best in the arena, and has at length fallen at the feet of his adversary, disarmed and broken down in helplessness. There he lies, unable to strike a blow or lift his arm. He is stripped and stunned, disarmed and disabled, and there is nothing left for him but to lie at the feet of his adversary and appeal to him for mercy.

Now this is the position to which God wants to bring us, where we shall cease our struggles and our attempts at self-defense or self-improvement and throw ourselves helplessly upon the mercy of God. This is the sinner's only hope, and when he thus lies at the feet of mercy, Jesus is ready to lift him up and give him that free salvation which is waiting for all.

This, too, is the greatest need of the Christian who seeks a deeper and higher life—to come to a full realization of his nothingness and helplessness and to lie down, stripped and stunned, at the feet of Jesus.

Denying ungodliness—Titus 2:12.

L et us say no to the flesh, the world and the love of self, and learn the holy self-denial of which so much of the life of obedience consists. We must make no provision for the flesh, give no recognition to our lower life. We must say no to everything earthly and selfish. How very much of the life of faith consists in simply denying ourselves.

We begin with one great *yes* to God, and then we conclude with an eternal *no* to ourselves, the world, the flesh and the devil.

Nearly every commandment of the Decalogue is a *Thou shalt not.* In First Corinthians 13, with its beautiful picture of love, most of the characteristics of love are in the negative—what love does not, thinks not, says not, is not. And so you will find that the largest part of the life of consecration is really saying no.

> I am not my own,
> I belong to Him.
> I am His alone,
> I belong to Him.

Let us not be weary in well-doing
—Galatians 6:9.

If Paul could only know the consolation and hope that he has ministered to the countless generations who have marched along the pathway from the cross to the kingdom above! He would be willing to go through a thousand lives and a thousand deaths such as he endured for the blessing that has followed since his noble head rolled in the dust by the Ostian Gate of Rome.

And if the least of us could only anticipate the eternal issues that will probably spring from our humblest services of faith, we should only count our sacrifices and labors unspeakable heritages of honor and opportunity. We would cease to speak of trials and sacrifices made for God.

The smallest grain of faith is a deathless and incorruptible germ that will yet plant the heavens and cover the earth with harvest of imperishable glory. Let us lift up our heads, for the horizon is wider than the little circle we can see. We are living, we are suffering, we are laboring, we are trusting for the ages yet to come!

Who shall separate us from the love of Christ?—Romans 8:35.

W ho shall separate us from the love of Christ? After all the possible obstacles and enemies have been mentioned, one by one, the triumphant answer comes: *In all these things we are more than conquerors through him that loved us* (v. 37). Our trials will be turned to helps; our enemies will be taken prisoners and made to fight our battles. Like the weights that keep the tall pendulum clock going, so our very difficulties will prove incentives to faith and prayer and occasions for God's becoming more real to us. We shall acquire from our troubles not only deliverance but triumph, and in all these things we shall be even more than conquerors through Him who loved us.

Our security depends not upon our unchanging love but on the love of God in Christ Jesus toward us. It is not the clinging arms of the baby that keep it from falling, but the strong arms of the loving mother. God loves us with an everlasting love, and although all else may change He will never leave us, never forsake us.

Touched with the feeling of our infirmities—Hebrews 4:15.

Some of us know a little what it is to be affected with a sense of the sufferings, and sometimes the sins, of others—sins, as they come into contact with us, that seem to saturate us and throw over us an awful sense of need.

Perhaps this is intended to give us some faint conception of the sympathy that Jesus felt when He had taken our sins, our sicknesses and our sorrows. Let us not hesitate to lay them on Him! It is far easier for Him to bear them than for us to bear them. He has already borne them for us, both in His life and in His death.

Let us roll the burden upon Jesus and let it roll away. Then, strong in His strength and rested in His life and love, let us go forth to minister to others the sympathy and help which He has so richly given us. The world is full of sorrow, and they that have known its bitterness and healing are God's ministers of consolation to a weeping world.

> Oh, the tears that flow around us.
> Let us wipe them while we may;
> Bring the broken hearts to Jesus,
> He will wipe their tears away.

How long halt ye between two opinions?
—*1 Kings 18:21.*

It is strange that people will not get over the idea that a consecrated life is a difficult one. A simple illustration will answer this foolish impression. Suppose a streetcar operator were to say, "It is much easier to run with one wheel on the track and the other off." His line would soon be dropped by the public, who would prefer to walk. Of course, it is ever so much easier to run with both wheels on the track—and always on the track—and it is much easier to follow Christ fully than to follow Him with a half heart and halting step. Elijah was right in his pungent question, *How long halt ye between two opinions?* The undecided man is a halting man. The halting man is a lame man and a miserable man, but the out-and-out Christian is the admiration of men and angels and a continual joy to himself.

> Say, is it all for Jesus,
> As you so often sing?
> Is He your Royal Master,
> Is He your heart's true King?

······································

First gave their own selves to the Lord,
and unto us by the will of God
—2 Corinthians 8:5.

In order to be successful in Christian work, it is essential that a person be loyal not only to God but to the work with which he or she is associated. The more deeply a person knows the Lord, the easier it is for him to get along with others.

Superficial Christians are apt to be eccentric. Mature Christians are so near the Lord that they are not afraid of missing His guidance. They are not always trying to promote their loyalty to God by their independence from others.

The Corinthians, who had given themselves first to the Lord, had no difficulty in giving themselves to His apostle by the will of God. It is delightful to work with true hearts who can be utterly depended upon. May God give us the spirit of a sound mind and a heart to "help along."

> You can help by holy prayer,
> Helpful love and joyful song;
> Oh, the burdens you may bear;
> Oh, the sorrows you may share;
> Oh, the crowns you may yet wear,
> If you help along.

Now it is high time to awake out of sleep; . . . let us therefore cast off the works of darkness, and let us put on the armour of light—Romans 13:11-12.

Let us wake out of sleep, let us be alert, let us be alive to the great necessities that really concern us.

Let us put off the garments of the night and the indulgences of the night, the loose robes of pleasure and the flowing garments of repose. The festal pleasures of the hours of darkness are not for the children of the day. Let us cast off the works of darkness.

Let us arm ourselves for the day. As we put on our clothes let us put on our weapons, for we are stepping out into a land of enemies and a world of dangers. Let us put on the helmet of salvation, the breastplate of righteousness and the shield of faith. Let us stand armed and vigilant as the dangers of the last days gather around us.

Let us put on the Lord Jesus Christ. He is our robe of day—not our own works or righteousness, but the person and righteousness of the Lord Jesus Christ, who gave us His very life and becomes to us our All-Sufficiency.

Go out into the highways and hedges,
and compel them to come in—Luke 14:2.

In the parable in Luke 14 of the great supper an ancient lord prepared for his friends and neighbors, there is a significant picture and object lesson of the program of Christianity in this age.

In the first place, it is obvious to every thoughtful mind that the Master is hearing an increasing number of excuses from the gospel-hardened people of Christian countries. It is becoming increasingly more difficult to interest the unsaved of our own land, especially those who have been accustomed to hearing the gospel, in the things of Christ. They have asked to be excused from the feast, and the Lord is turning from them.

At the same time two remarkable alternatives indicated in the parable are becoming more and more manifest. One is the movement to take the gospel to the slums and the neglected classes at home; the other is the movement to take the gospel to the neglected classes abroad.

Behold, I am the Lord, the god of all flesh: is there anything too hard for me?—Jeremiah 32:27.

Cyrus the king was compelled to fulfill the vision of Jeremiah by making a decree declaring that Jehovah had bidden him rebuild Jerusalem and invite her captives to return to their native home. In this way Jeremiah's faith was vindicated and Jehovah's prophecy gloriously fulfilled, as faith ever will be honored. Oh, for the faith that in the dark present and the darkest future shall dare to subscribe the evidences and seal up the documents for the time of waiting and then begin to testify to its hope like the prophet of Anathoth!

The word Anathoth has a beautiful meaning: echoes. So faith is the echo of God, and He always gives the echo to faith as he answers it in glorious fulfillment. Let our faith echo also the brave claim of the ancient prophet and take our full inheritance with his glorious shout, "O Lord, Thou art the God of all flesh, is there anything too hard for [thee]?" Back like an echo will come the heavenly assurance to our hearts, "For the *God of all flesh*: nothing is too hard."

Thou good servant: because thou hast been faithful in a very little, have thou authority over ten cities
—Luke 19:17.

It is not our success in service that counts, but our fidelity. Caleb and Joshua were faithful and God remembered their faithfulness when the day of visitation came. For them it was a very difficult and unpopular position. For us, too. We are called in the crises of our lives to stand alone. In the very matter of trusting God for victory over sin and our full inheritance in Christ we all have to be tested as they.

Even in the Church of God our brethren, while admitting in the abstract the loveliness and advantages of life in Christ, tell us that it is impracticable and impossible. Many of us have had to stand alone for years witnessing to the power of Christ to save His people to the uttermost. Like Joshua and Caleb, we have had to follow God alone as we followed Him wholly. But this is the real victory of faith and the proof of our uncompromising fidelity.

Let us not, therefore, complain when we suffer reproach for our testimony or stand alone for God. Let us, rather, thank Him that He so honors us and stand the test so that He can afterwards use us when the multitudes are glad to follow.

....

Whatsoever ye shall ask the Father in
my name, he will give it you
—John 16:23.

Two men go to the bank cashier, both holding in their hands a piece of paper. One is dressed expensively and presents a gloved and jeweled hand. The other is a rough, unwashed workman. The first is rejected with a polite sentence; the second receives a thousand dollars over the counter.

What was the difference? The one presented a worthless name; the other handed in a note endorsed by the president of the bank. Just so, the most virtuous moralist will be turned away from the gates of mercy and the vilest sinner, if he presents the name of Jesus, welcomed in.

What shall we give to infinite purity and righteousness? Jesus! No other gift is worthy for God to receive. And He has given Him to us for this very end, to give back as our substitute and satisfaction. And God has "testified" of this gift what He has of no other: in Him He is well pleased, and all who receive Him are *accepted in the beloved* (Ephesians 2:6). Shall we accept the testimony that God is satisfied with His Son? Shall we be satisfied with Him?

Dwell deep—Jeremiah 49:8.

God's presence blends with every other thought and consciousness, flowing sweetly and evenly through our business plans, our social interactions, our hearts' affections, our manual toil, our entire lives. Like the fragrance of a flower or the presence of a friend consciously near, and yet not hindering in the least the most intense and constant preoccupation of the hands and brain, so God consecrates all and is conscious through all. How beautiful the established habit of this unceasing communion and dependence amid and above all thoughts and occupations! How lovely to see a dear old saint folding away his books at night and humbly saying, "Lord Jesus, things are still just the same between us" and then falling asleep in His keeping.

So let us be stayed upon Him. Let us grow into Him with all the roots and fibers of our beings. He will not get tired of our friendship. He will not want to put us off sometimes. Beautiful words of the suffering saint: "He never says goodbye." He stays. So let us be stayed on Him.

My grace is sufficient for thee: for my strength is made perfect in weakness —2 Corinthians 12:9.

God allowed the crisis that closed around Jacob, on the night when he bowed at Peniel in supplication, to bring him to the place where he could take hold of God as he never would have done. From that narrow pass of peril Jacob came, enlarged in his faith and knowledge of God and in the power of a new and victorious life.

God had to compel David, by a long and painful discipline of years, to learn the almighty power and faithfulness of his God, and to grow up into the established principles of faith and godliness which were indispensable for his subsequent and glorious career as the king of Israel.

Nothing but the extremities in which Paul was constantly placed could ever have taught him, and taught the Church through him, the full meaning of the great promise he so learned to claim, *My grace is sufficient for thee.* And nothing but our trials and perils would ever have led some of us to know Him as we do, to trust Him as we have and to draw from Him the measures of grace which our very extremities made indispensable.

We will come unto him, and make our abode with him—John 14:23.

The idea of trying to obtain a holiness of our own, and then having Christ reward us for it, is not His teaching. Oh, no. Christ is the holiness. He Himself, the Holy One, will come to dwell in the heart forever.

When a millionaire buys a piece of property with an old shanty on it, he does not fix up the old shanty. He contracts with someone to tear it down. In its place he then builds a mansion. We are not to try to fix up the old shanty; rather, we are to give Christ the property. He will excavate below our old life and build a suitable house where He will live forever.

That is what we mean when we say that Christ will be the preparation for the blessing of holiness and make way for His own approach. Picture a great Assyrian king setting out on a march. He did not command the people to make a road, but he sent his own men on ahead to cut down the trees, fill the ravines and level the mountains. So, if we will let Him, will Christ be the Coming King, the Author and Finisher of our faith.

....

Bringing into captivity every thought
to the obedience of Christ
—2 Corinthians 10:5.

If we would abide in Christ we must have no confidence in self. Self-repression must be ever the prime necessity of divine fullness and efficiency. How quickly we want to spring to the front when any emergency arises. When something in which we are interested comes up, we say what we think under some sudden impulse. Then perhaps there are weeks of taking back our thoughts and taking the Lord's instead.

It is only when we get out of the way of the Lord that He can use us. So, let us leave self behind us, always suspending our will about everything until we have looked at the issue and said: "Lord, what is Your will? What is Your thought about it?"

Those who thus abide in Christ have the habit of reserve and quiet; they are not rattling and reckless talkers, they will not always have an opinion about everything—and they will not always know what they are going to do. There will be a deferential holding back of judgment and walking softly with God. It is our headlong, impulsive spirit that keeps us so constantly from hearing and following the Lord.

···

This is my beloved, and this is my friend—Song of Solomon 5:16.

God is our friend. *Which of you shall have a friend, . . . at midnight?* asked Jesus (Luke 11:5). This concept of God as our friend has deep significance for each one of us. Who has not had a friend, who in some respects was more of a friend than anyone in the family? Reflect upon that friendship. Recall each act of love. Think of all you could trust that friend to do for you and all the ways in which he or she stood by you. Then as you concentrate the whole weight of recollection and affection, put God in that place of confidence and realize He is all that friend has been and infinitely more.

Our Friend! The one who is personally interested in us, who has set His heart upon us, who has come near to us in the tender and delicate intimacy of unspeakable fellowship. He has given us invaluable pledges and promises, He has done very much for us, He is ever ready to go to any trouble or expense to aid us. To Him we come in prayer—our heavenly Friend.

Hath the Lord as great delight in burnt offerings and sacrifices, as in obeying the voice of the Lord?—1 Samuel 15:22.

Many a person prays for sanctification but fails to enter into the blessing because he does not intelligently understand and faithfully accept God's appointed means—Jesus Christ and the indwelling of the Spirit. Many a prayer for the salvation of others is hindered because the very friend who has prayed takes the wrong course to bring about the answer and resorts to means which defeat his object.

There are wives pleading for the salvation of their husbands who hope to win them by avoiding anything that may offend them, yielding to all their worldly tastes in the hope of attracting them to Christ. Far more effective would be an attitude of fidelity to God and fearless testimony to their husbands, such as God could bless.

Many a congregation wonders why it is so poor and struggling. It may be because its financial methods are wholly unscriptural and unworthy of even ordinary self-respect.

When we ask God for any blessing, we must allow Him to direct the steps which are to bring the answer.

....

I in them, and thou in me—John 17:23.

If we would be enlarged to the full measure of God's purpose, let us endeavor to realize something of our own capacities for His filling.

We little know the size of a human soul and spirit. Never, until He renews, cleanses and enters the heart, can we have any adequate conception of the possibilities of the being whom God made in His very image, and whom He now renews after the pattern of the Lord Jesus Himself.

We know, however, that God has made the human soul to be His temple and abode. God knows how to make the house that can hold His infinite fullness. We know something of this as all our nature quickens into springtime life at the coming of the Holy Spirit. We know it as from time to time new baptisms awaken the dormant powers and susceptibilities that we did not realize we possessed.

Let us give God the right to make the best of us. Filled with wonder, we shall some day behold the glorious temple that He has built and say, *Lord, what is man, that thou art mindful of him?* (Psalm 8:4).

Bless the Lord, O my soul
—Psalm 103:1.

B *less the Lord, O my soul: and all that is within* *me, bless his holy name. Bless the Lord, O my* *soul, and forget not all his benefits: who forgiveth all* *thine iniquities; who healeth all thy diseases; who* *redeemeth thy life from destruction; who crowneth thee* *with lovingkindness and tender mercies; who satisfieth* *thy mouth with good things; so that thy youth is re-* *newed like the eagle's* (vv.1-5).

Who so well can sing this thanksgiving song as we who rejoice in God's full salvation and praise God for the glorious health of a risen Lord and a continual youth?

This psalm and its opening verses is in the very center of the Scriptures by an exact count of letters and verses. So let it stand central in our lives, as we look backward and forward and upward in grateful thanksgiving. Let us sing in the words of its closing strains, *Bless the Lord, all* *his works in all places of his dominion: bless the Lord,* *O my soul* (Psalm 103:22). Lord, center my heart in Thee and in the spirit of love and praise.

> *I will strengthen thee; yea, I will help thee; yea, I will uphold thee*
> *—Isaiah 41:10.*

God has three ways of helping us. First, He says, *I will strengthen thee.* In other words, He is saying, "I will make you a little stronger yourself." Second, He adds, *I will help thee.* By that we understand Him to say, "I will add my strengh to your strength, but you shall lead and I will help you." Third, He says, *I will uphold thee with the right hand of my righteousness*—or, "I will lift you up bodily and carry you altogether. It will be neither your strength nor My help, but My complete upholding."

When we come to the end of our strength, we come to the beginning of His. In Him the weakest are the strongest, and the most helpless the most helped. *He giveth power to the faint,* but to *them that have no might* at all *He increaseth strength.* His word forever is, *My grace is sufficient for thee.*

The answer is a paradox of contradictions, and yet the most practical of truths.

Most gladly therefore will I rather glory in my infirmities, that the power of Christ may rest upon me. . . . For when I am weak, then am I strong (2 Corinthians 12:9-10).

For the law of the Spirit of life in Christ Jesus hath made me free—Romans 8:2.

There is a natural law of sin and sickness. If we just sink into the trend of circumstances we shall go down and sink under the power of the tempter. But there is another law of spiritual life and physical life in Christ Jesus to which we can rise and through which we can counterbalance and overcome the law that bears us down. But to do this requires real spiritual energy, fixed purpose and a settled posture and habit of faith.

In the factory that relies on a single source of mechanical power, it is necessary to engage the belt that turns the central shaft and keeps it engaged. The power is there, but only if the connection is maintained is it usable power to operate the machinery.

There is a spiritual law of choosing, believing, abiding and holding steady in our walk with God that is essential to the working of the Holy Spirit either in our sanctification or healing.

> There is a word that saves the soul,
> "I will trust";
> It makes the sick and suffering whole,
> "I will trust."

Because I live, ye shall live also
—John 14:19.

After having become adjusted to our Living Head and the source of our life, our business now is to abide, absorb and grow. We do this by leaning on Christ's strength, drinking in His life, feeding on Him as the Living Bread and drawing all of our resources from Him in continual dependence and communion.

The Holy Spirit will be the great Teacher and Minister in this blessed process. He will take of the things of Christ and show them to us, and He will impart them through all the channels and functions of our spiritual lives. As we yield ourselves to Him He will breathe His own prayer of communion, drawing out our hearts in longings and hungerings, which are the pledge of their own fulfillment, calling us apart in silent and wordless prayer, and opening every sense and sensibility of our spiritual beings to take in His life.

As the lungs absorb the oxygen from the atmosphere, as the senses breathe in the sweet odors of the garden, so the heart instinctively receives and rejoices in the affection and fellowship of the beloved One by our sides. Thus each of us becomes *like a tree planted by the rivers of water* (Psalm 1:3).

··

*But prayer was made without ceasing of
the church unto God for him
—Acts 12:5.*

*B*ut *prayer* is the link that connects us with
God. It is the bridge that spans every gulf
and bears us over every abyss of danger or of
need. How significant the picture of the
apostolic church: Peter in prison, the Jews
triumphant, Herod supreme, the arena of martyrdom awaiting the dawning of the morning to
drink up the apostle's blood—everything
against it. *But prayer was made without ceasing of the
church unto God for him.* And what was the se-
quel? The prison open, the apostle free, the
Jews baffled, the wicked king eaten of worms—
a spectacle of hideous retribution—and the
Word of God rolling on in greater victory.

Do we know the power of our supernatural
weapon? Do we dare to use it with the authority of a faith that commands as well as asks?
May God baptize us with holy audacity and
divine confidence. He is not wanting great men
and women, but He is wanting men and women
who will dare to prove the greatness of their
God.

But God! *But prayer!*

Reckon ye also yourselves to be dead indeed—Romans 6:11.

O ur life from the dead is to be followed up by the habit and attitude which is the logical outcome of all this. *Reckon ye also yourselves to be dead indeed unto sin, but alive unto God through Jesus Christ . . . but yield yourselves unto God,* not to die over again every day, but *as those that are alive from the dead, and your members as instruments of righteousness unto God* (Romans 6:11, 13).

Further, Christ's resurrection life is given to fit us for *the fellowship of his sufferings, being made conformable unto his death* (Philippians 3:10).

It is intended to enable us to toil and suffer with rejoicing and victory. We *mount up with wings as eagles* that we may *run, and not be weary; . . . walk, and not faint* (Isaiah 40:31).

But let us not mistake the sufferings. They do not mean our sufferings, but His. They are not our struggles after holiness, our sicknesses and pains, but those higher sufferings which, with Him, we bear for others and for a suffering Church and a dying world. May God help us not to sorrow for ourselves, but put us at leisure, in the power of His resurrection, to bear His burdens and drink His cup.

The earnest of the Spirit in our hearts
—2 Corinthians 1:22.

Life in earnest—what a rare, what a glorious spectacle! We see it in the Son of God; we see it in His apostle; we see it in every noble, consecrated and truly successful life. Without it there may be a thousand good things, but they lack the golden thread that binds them all into a chain of power and permanence. They are like costly and beautiful beads, that fall in confusion from a broken string, and are lost in the end for want of the bond that alone could bind them into a life of consistent and lasting power.

Oh, for the baptism of fire! Oh, for the earnest, the Spirit! Oh, for lives that have but one thing to do or care for! Oh, for the depth and everlasting strength of the heart of Christ within us, to love, to sacrifice, to realize, to persevere, to live and die like Him!

> We are going forth with a trust
> so sacred,
> And a truth so divine and deep,
> With a message clear and a work
> so glorious,
> And a charge—such a charge—to keep.
> Let it be your greatest joy,
> my brother,
> That the Lord can count on you:
> And if all besides should fail and falter,
> To your trust be always true.

···

Delight thyself also in the Lord
—Psalm 37:4.

Daniel's heart was filled with God's love for His work and kingdom, and his prayers were the mightiest forces of his time. Through them God gave to him the restoration of Israel to their own land, and the acknowledgment by the rulers of the world of the God of whom he testified and for whom he lived.

There is a beautiful promise in Psalm 37: *Delight thyself also in the Lord; and he shall give thee the desires of thine heart* (v.4). It is, perhaps, legitimate to translate this as meaning not only the fulfillment of our desires, but even the inspiration of our desires, the inbreathing of His thoughts into us so that our prayers shall be in accord with His will and bring back to us the unfailing answer of His mighty providence.

> Teach me Thy thoughts, O God!
> Think Thou, Thyself, in me;
> Then shall I only always think
> Thine own thoughts after Thee.
>
> Teach me Thy thoughts, O God!
> Show me Thy plan divine;
> Save me from all my plans and works,
> And lead me into Thine.

The things which are seen are temporal
—2 Corinthians 4:18.

How strong is the snare of the things that are seen, and how necessary for God to keep us in the things that are unseen! If Peter is to walk on the water, he must walk; if he is going to swim, he must swim; but he cannot do both. If the bird is going to fly it must keep away from the fences and the trees and trust to its buoyant wings. If it tries to keep within easy reach of the ground, it will make poor work of flying.

God had to bring Abraham to the end of his own strength and to let him see that in his own body he could do nothing. He had to consider his own body as good as dead and then take God for the whole work. When he looked away from himself and trusted God alone, then he became fully persuaded that what God had promised He was able also to perform.

This is what God is teaching us. He has to withhold encouraging results until we learn to trust without them, and then He loves to make His work real in fact as well as faith.

Let us look only to Him today to do *what* He will choose *in the way* He will choose.

....

O man of desires (margin)—Daniel 10:11.

O man of desires was the divine character given to Daniel. The thought is translated in the King James version, *A man greatly beloved*. But it literally means, *O man of desires*. Desire is a necessary element in all spiritual forces. It is one of the secrets of effectual prayer. *What things soever ye desire, when ye pray, believe that ye receive them* (Mark 11:24). The element of strong desire gives momentum to our purposes and prayers. Indifference is an unwholesome condition; indolence and apathy are offensive both to God and nature.

So it is in our spiritual lives: God often has to wake us up by the presence of trying circumstances and push us into new places of trust by forces that we must subdue.

There is no factor in prayer more effectual than love. If we are intensely interested in an object or an individual, our petitions become like living forces. Not only do they convey their wants to God, but in some sense they convey God's help back to us.

May God so fill us today with the heart of Christ that we may glow with the divine fire of holy desire.

*Watch therefore, for ye know neither
the day nor the hour—Matthew 25:13.*

Jesus illustrates the unexpectedness of His coming by the figure of a thief entering a house when the master is not there. Life, like the old Jewish night, may be divided into three watches—youth, maturity, old age. The summons to meet God may come to us in any of these watches.

A writer tells us of his experience with a camping party of which he was a member and which, he tells us, always arranged to have watches at night. "We became especially careful after what I am about to narrate happened. During the first night, from sunset to sunrise, we had in turn carefully guarded our camp. But when the next night came, we were so impressed with the seeming safety of the neighborhood that we concluded no guard was needed until bedtime. We spent the evening in the main tent— telling stories, singing and enjoying ourselves. When the hour to retire arrived, we discovered that our other tents had been robbed and everything of value stolen. The mischief was done before we thought a guard necessary."

It is never too soon to begin watching against sin.

....

The ark of the covenant of the Lord
went before them—Numbers 10:33.

God does give us impressions but not with the intent that we should act on them as impressions. If the impression comes from God, He will Himself give sufficient evidence to establish it beyond the possibility of a doubt.

We read of the impression that came to Jeremiah concerning the purchase of the field of Anathoth. Jeremiah, however, did not act upon this impression until after the following day, when his uncle's son came to him and brought him external evidence by making a proposal for the purchase. Then Jeremiah said, *I knew that this was the word of the Lord* (Jeremiah 32:8).

He waited until God seconded the impression by a providence, and then he acted in full view of the open facts that could bring conviction unto others as well as himself.

God wants us to act according to His mind. We are not to ignore the Shepherd's personal voice, but like Paul and his companions at Troas we are to listen to all the voices that speak and gather from all the circumstances, as they did, the full mind of the Lord.

And he that sat upon the throne said,
. . . It is done—Revelation 21:5, 6.

Great is the difference between action and transaction. We may be constantly acting without accomplishing anything, but a transaction is action that passes beyond the point of return and becomes a permanent committal.

Salvation is a transaction between the soul and Christ in which the matter passes beyond recall. Sanctification is a great transaction in which we are utterly surrendered, irrevocably consecrated and wholly committed to the Holy Spirit; then He comes and seals the transaction and undertakes the work. Our covenant for our Lord's healing should be just as explicit, definite and irrevocable.

This should also be true of the covenants to which God is leading His children from time to time in regard to other matters of obedience and service. God grant that during this hallowed day many a consecrated life may be able to say with new significance and permanence, " 'Tis done, the great transaction's done."

> For the living Vine is Jesus;
> In whose fullness we may hide;
> And find our life and fruitfulness
> As we in Him abide.

·······································

We would see Jesus—John 12:21.

When any great blessing is awaiting us, the devil is sure to try to make it so disagreeable to us that we shall miss it. It is a good thing to know Satan as a liar and to remember, when he is trying to prejudice us strongly against any cause, that very likely the greatest blessing of our lives lies there. Spurgeon once said that the best evidence that God was on our side is the devil's growl, and we are generally pretty safe in following a thing according to Satan's dislike for it.

Take care lest, in the very line where your prejudices are setting you apart from God's people and God's truth, you are missing the treasures of your life. Take the treasures of heaven no matter how they come to you, even if, as earthly treasures generally are, they are like the kernel inside the rough shell or the gem in the center of the hard rock.

> I have seen Jesus, and my heart is
>   dead to all beside,
> I have seen Jesus, and my wants are all,
>   in Him, supplied.
> I have seen Jesus, and my heart, at last,
>   is satisfied,
> Since I've seen Jesus.

··

The disciple whom Jesus loved . . . leaned on his breast—John 21:20.

An American gentleman once visited the saintly Albert Bengel. He was very desirous to hear him pray. So one night he lingered at his door, hoping to overhear his closing devotions. The rooms were adjoining and the doors ajar. The good man finished his studies, closed his books, knelt down for a moment and simply said, "Dear Lord Jesus, things are still the same between us" and then quietly fell asleep. So close was his communion with his Lord that labor did not interrupt it and prayer was not necessary to renew it. It was a ceaseless, almost unconscious presence, like the fragrance of the summer garden or the company of some special person by our side whose presence we somehow feel, even though the busy hours pass by and not a word is exchanged.

> O blessed fellowship, divine,
> O joy, supremely sweet,
> Companionship with Jesus here,
> Makes life with joy replete;
> O wondrous grace, O joy sublime,
> I've Jesus with me all the time.

....

*Consider the lilies of the field, how
they grow—Matthew 6:28.*

It is said that a mother found her small boy
standing beside a tall sunflower, with his feet
stuck in the ground. When she asked, "What in
the world are you doing there?" he naively
answered, "Why, I am trying to grow to be a
man."

His mother laughed heartily at the idea of his
being planted in the ground in order to grow like
the sunflower. Then, patting him gently on the
head, she said, "Why, Harry, that is not the way
to grow. You can never grow bigger by trying.
Just come right in and eat enough good food and
have plenty of play and you will soon grow to be
a man without trying so hard."

Harry's mother was right. There could not be
a better answer to the question: "How do the
lilies grow?" than Hannah Whitehall Smith's
comment, "They grow without trying."

Our deepest spiritual life is the life of self-
unconsciousness through which we become
united to Christ. We live continually on His
life, being nourished, fed and constantly filled
with His Spirit and presence and all the fullness
of His imparted life.

Cast out the beam out of thine own eye
—Matthew 7:5.

Greater than the fault we condemn and criticize is the sin of criticism and condemnation. There is no time that demands such grace as when we deal with an erring one.

A lady once called on me on her way to give an erring sister a piece of her mind. I advised her to wait until she could love the woman a little more. Only Jesus, who loved sinners well enough to die for them, can deal with the erring. We can never see all the heart. He does, and He can convict without condemning and reprove without discouraging.

Oh, for more of the heart of Christ! Take care how you speak of another's fault. Some day soon you may be in the same or deeper condemnation. Very significantly does the Master say that the man who sees a mote in his brother's eye usually has a rafter in his own.

> Give me a heart like Thine,
> Give me a heart like Thine.
> By Thy wonderful power,
> By Thy grace every hour,
> Give me a heart like Thine.

It is high time to awake out of sleep
—Romans 13:11.

One of the greatest enemies to faith is indolence. It is much easier to lie and suffer than to rise and overcome. It is much easier to go to sleep on a snowbank and never wake again than to rouse one's self and shake off the lethargy and overcome the stupor. Faith is an energetic art. Prayer is intense labor. The effectual working prayer of the righteous man availeth much.

Satan tries to put us to sleep as he did the disciples in the garden. Let us not sleep as do others, but let us awake and be sober, continuing in prayer and *watching thereunto with all perseverance* (Ephesians 6:18), stirring up ourselves to take hold of God's strength, *not slothful, but followers of them who through faith and patience inherit the promise* (Hebrews 6:12).

It is the wind that carries the sailing ship across the waves, but the wind is powerless unless the hand of the boatman is held firmly upon the rudder and the rudder set hard against the wind. In like manner we hold the rudder; God fills the sails. It is not the rudder that carries the ship, but it is the rudder turned against the wind that carries the ship. So God keeps us in *perfect peace* while we are *stayed upon Him* (Isaiah 26:3).

I can do all things through Christ
—Philippians 4:13.

A woman remarked in my hearing: "I have so much work to do that I haven't time to wait on the Lord to get strength to do it." Surely that was making bricks without straw. Even if her tasks were in the name of the Lord and the church, she was under the devil's bondage.

God sends not His servants on their own charges; but *God is able to make all grace abound toward you; that ye, always having all sufficiency in all things, may abound unto every good work* (2 Corinthians 9:8).

The old Latin motto *festina lente*—"Make haste slowly"—has a great lesson for us. The more work we have to do, the more frequently we must drop our heads upon our desks and wait a moment for heavenly aid and love. Then we can press on with new strength. One hour baptized in the love of the Holy Spirit is worth ten battling against wind and tide without the heavenly life.

> I dwell with the King for His work,
> And the work, it is His and not mine;
> He plans and prepares it for me
> And fills me with power divine.
> So duty is changed to delight,
> And prayer into praise as I sing;
> I dwell with my King for His work
> And work in the strength of my King.

*Judge nothing before the time, until
the Lord come—1 Corinthians 4:5.*

Nothing will more effectually arrest the
working of the Spirit in the heart than
the spirit of criticism. At the end of a meeting, a
young minister came forward and told me of the
great blessing he had received that afternoon
and of the baptism of the Holy Spirit that had
come into his heart and being, setting him free
from the bondage of years. And then he added,
"It all came through your answer to that
question, 'Will a criticizing spirit hinder the
Holy Spirit from filling the heart?'"

As the question was asked and answered, he
said, "I was sitting in the church criticizing much
of what was going on, objecting to this thing and
to that thing, finding fault with the expressions
of praise and testimony and feeling thoroughly
unhappy. The Lord brought the answer home to
my heart and convicted me of my sin. There and
then I laid it down and began to see the good
instead of the evil. Blessing fell upon me, and my
soul was filled with joy and praise. I saw where
my error lay—that for years I had been trying to
see the truth with my head instead of my heart."

As my Father hath sent me, even so send I you—John 20:21.

Preeminent above all other ministries for the evangelization of the heathen world is the Great Commission. The command, *Go ye into all the world, and preach the gospel to every creature* (Luke 16:15), requires a personal ministry from *man to man* and for *every man*. The command to begin *at Jerusalem* passes on to us the obligation to reach God's chosen people. *Go ye . . . and disciple all nations* raises our commission to a nobler plane and makes us ambassadors for the King of kings and trustees of the gospel for every kindred and tribe and tongue. The command, *Ye shall be witnesses unto me both in Jerusalem, and in all Judaea, and in Samaria, and unto the uttermost part of the earth* (Acts 1:8), lifts the outlook beyond any section of humanity, any circle of selfish patriotism and any form of religious selfishness. It makes the work of evangelization the one supreme ministry of the Church of Christ and the one paramount responsibility of every disciple of the Lord Jesus Christ.

Have you come into close touch with the risen Christ or caught the spirit of His last momentous days on earth? If so, you cannot be inactive, indifferent or even neutral in this mighty enterprise which is the emergency work of our times and which is the one great business for which God has called us.

And the Lord had respect unto Abel and his offering—Genesis 4:4.

The two men who stand worshiping at the gate of Eden represent the two divisions of mankind—believers and unbelievers.

The earthly man has far more beauty, culture and real effort in his religion. He brings the first and best of the rich, ripe produce of summer. Perhaps his altar is in favorable contrast to the rude mound of clay on which Abel offers the ghastly and revolting sacrifice of a bleeding, dying lamb.

Cain's whole offering was a direct denial of what God had said about the curse upon the ground and its fruits, of the fact of sin and the need of an atoning Savior. Abel's sacrifice acknowledged this truth and accepted God's way of pardon.

The first act of faith is to believe what God says about sin—to believe that we are sinners because God says it. Abel did. He took the sinner's place and instantly found the sinner's Savior. Cain would not see his sin and as a result, fell into deeper sin.

The devil tricks us into saying, "I have not sinned." Humble faith accepts God's judgment upon sin and thereby escapes its penalty.

Without me ye can do nothing
—John 15:5.

How much can we do for Christ? We are accustomed to say, "As much as I can." Have we ever thought that we can do more than we can?

This thought was lately suggested by the remarks of a Christian friend who told how God had laid it upon her heart to do something for His cause which was beyond her power. When she dared to obey Him, He gave her the assurance of His power and resources. So marvelously did He meet her faith that she was enabled to do more than she could have otherwise. She was able to accomplish her heart's desire and see a work fulfilled to which her resources were unequal.

The apostle says, *I can do all things through Christ, which strengtheneth me,* and yet He says we are not able to *think anything, as of ourselves* (2 Corinthians 3:5).

Oh, blessed sufficiency! Oh, blessed All-Sufficiency! Oh blessed nothingness, which brings us all things! Oh, blessed faith, whose rich dowry is, *All things are possible to him that believeth!*

> Oh, to be found of Him in peace,
> Spotless and free from blame.

Could ye not watch with me one hour?—Matthew 26:40.

A young woman whose parents had died while she was an infant had been cared for by a friend of the family. Before she was old enough to know him he went to Europe. Through all his years of absence he wrote regularly to her and never failed to send her money for all her wants.

Finally word came that during a certain week he would return and visit her. He did not fix the day or the hour. During that week the young woman received several invitations to take pleasant trips with her friends. One of these sounded so exciting that she could not resist accepting it. But during her trip her benefactor came, inquired as to her absence and left. Returning she found a note:

"My life," the note said, "has been a struggle for you; might you not have waited one week for me?" More she never heard, and her life of plenty became one of want.

Jesus has not fixed the day or hour of His return but He has said, *Watch.* Should He come today, would He find us absorbed in thoughtless dissipation? May we be found each day in the expectant attitude of those watching for a loved one.

....

In lowliness of mind let each esteem
other better than themselves
—Philippians 2:3.

When the apostle speaks of *the deep things of God* (1 Corinthians 2:10), he means more than deep spiritual truth. There must be something before this. There must be a deep soil and a thorough foundation.

Much of our spiritual teaching fails because the people to whom it is directed are so shallow. Their deeper nature has never been stirred.

The beatitudes begin at the bottom of things—the poor in spirit, the mourners, the hungry hearts. Suffering is essential to profound spiritual life. We need not go to a monastery or a hospital for the leprous to find it. Unless we are born into a different race than Adam's, the first real opportunity for unselfishness will bring into our lives the anguish of crucifixion.

Because men and women have not faced this truth, they know little of suffering and death. We must have deep convictions. Truth must be to us a necessity and principle a part of our very being.

Lord, make me poor in spirit. Help me to be even as Thou wert when on earth—always the lowest and, therefore, *highly exalted* (Philippians 2:9).

As he is, so are we in this world
—1 John 4:17.

Jesus will come into our surrendered lives and unite Himself with us, imparting to us His own life and being. From day to day, He will become the supply of our spiritual needs and the substitute for our helplessness.

Our part is simply to yield fully, recognizing our worthlessness, and then taking Jesus Himself to live in us and be, moment by moment, our strength and purity and victory.

> One in His death on the tree,
> One as He rose from the dead;
> I from the curse am as free
> E'en as my glorious Head.
>
> One in His merits I stand,
> One as I pray in His name,
> All that His worth can demand
> I may with confidence claim.
>
> All that He has shall be mine,
> All that He is I shall be;
> Robed in His glory divine,
> I shall be even as He.

Looking diligently lest any man fail
—Hebrews 12:15.

It is not losing all but coming short that we are to fear. We may not lose our souls, but we may lose something more precious than life—God's full approval, His highest choice and our incorruptible and star-gemmed crown. It is the one degree more that makes all the difference between hot water—powerless in the boiler—and steam.

> I want, in this short life of mine,
> As much as can be pressed
> Of service true for God and man;
> Help me to be my best.
>
> I want, among the victory throng,
> To have my name confessed;
> And hear my Master say at last,
> Well done, you did your best.
>
> Give me, O Lord, Thy highest choice;
> Let others take the rest;
> Their good things have no charm
>   for me,
> For I have got Thy best.

For I am now ready to be offered
—2 Timothy 4:6.

When a Roman soldier was told by his guide that if he insisted on taking a certain journey it would probably be fatal, he answered, "It is necessary for me to go; it is not necessary for me to live." That was depth. When we are convicted like that we shall amount to something.

The shallow nature lives in its impulses, its impressions, its intuitions, its instincts and very largely in its surroundings. The profound character looks beyond all these and moves steadily on, sailing past the storms and clouds into the clear sunshine which is always on the other side. It waits for the afterward that inverts sorrow, seeming defeat and failure. When God has deepened us, then He can give us His deeper truths, His profoundest secrets, His mightier trusts.

Lord, lead me into the depths of Thy life and save me from a shallow experience.

> On to broader fields of holy vision;
> On to loftier heights of faith and love;
> Onward, upward, apprehending wholly
> All for which He calls thee from above.

From me is thy fruit found
—Hosea 14:8.

Nothing hinders our advance more than the currents in life's stream that bear us in the old direction until habit makes change almost impossible. The remedy for this is to take Christ afresh to be our Alpha and Omega for a deeper, higher, divine experience. Then we must wait even for His conception of our desires and prayers, afraid lest our highest thought should be below His great plan of wisdom and love.

> Oh, Comforter gentle and tender,
> Oh, holy and heavenly Dove,
> We're yielding our hearts in surrender,
> We're waiting Thy fullness to prove.

> Anoint us with gladness and healing;
> Baptize us with power from on high;
> Oh, come with filling and sealing
> While low at Thy footstool we lie.

With a perfect heart . . . to make David king—1 Chronicles 12:38.

What is the supreme purpose of our lives? The Israelites were of one heart to make David king. Is this our purpose, to prepare the Bride, to prepare the world, to prepare His way?

Does this objective dwarf and dim all other ambitions, all other cares? Does it fill and satisfy every capacity, every power, every desire? Does it absorb every moment, every energy, every resource? Does it give direction and tone to every plan and work of life? Does it decide for us the education of our children, the investment of our means, the friendships and associations of life, the whole activity, interest and outlook of our beings? Are we in it, spirit, soul and body—all we are, all we do, all we hope for—of one heart to make Jesus King?

We're going forth united
With loyal heart and hand,
To bear His royal banner
Abroad o'er every land.

From every tribe and nation
We'll haste His Bride to bring,
And, oh, with what glad welcome
We'll make our Jesus King.

Humble yourselves therefore under the mighty hand of God, that he may exalt you—1 Peter 5:6.

Opposition is essential to a true equilibrium of forces. The centripetal and centrifugal forces acting in opposition to each other keep our planet in her orbit. The one propelling and the other repelling so act and react that instead of earth's being swept off into space in a pathway of desolation and destruction, she pursues her even orbit around her solar center.

So God guides our lives. It is not enough to have an impelling force—we need just as much a repelling force. For this reason, God holds us back by the testing ordeals of life, by the pressure of temptation and trial, by the things that seem to be against us but which really are furthering our way. He establishes our goings.

Let us thank God for both forces. Let us take the weights as well as the wings, and, thus divinely impelled, let us press on with faith and patience in our high and heavenly calling.

Lord, help me to learn from all that comes to me this day Thy highest will.

Abide with us: for it is toward evening
—Luke 24:29.

In his last messages to the disciples in John 14 and 15, the Lord Jesus clearly teaches us that the very essence of the highest holiness is *Abide in me, and I in you, . . . for without me ye can do nothing* (John 15:4-5).

The very purpose of the Holy Spirit whom Jesus promised was to reveal the Lord so that, in His own words, *at that day ye shall know that I am in my Father, and ye in me, and I in you* (John 14:20). The closing echo of His intercessory prayer was embraced in these three small but infinite words, "I in them."

> Is it for me to be cleansed by His power
> From the pollution of sin?
> Is it for me to be kept every hour
> By His abiding within?
>
> Wonderful promise so full and so free,
> Wonderful Savior, oh, how can it be—
> Cleansing and pardon and mercy
>   for me?
> Yes, it's for me, for me.

Is there no balm in Gilead; is there no physician there?—Jeremiah 8:22.

Divine healing is simply divine life. It is the headship of Christ over the body. It is the life of Christ within our frame. It is the union of our members with the very body of Christ and the inflowing life of Christ in our living members. It is as real as His risen and glorified body.

Divine healing is as reasonable as the fact that He was raised from the dead and is today a living man with a true body and a rational soul at God's right hand.

That living Christ belongs to us in all His attributes and powers. We are members of His body, His flesh and His bones. And if we can only believe it and receive it, we may live upon the very life of the Son of God.

Lord, help me to know *the body . . . for the Lord; and the Lord for the body.*

> There is healing in the promise,
> There is healing in the blood,
> There is strength for all our weakness
> In the risen Son of God.
>
> And the feeblest of His children
> All His glorious life may share;
> He has healing balm in Gilead,
> He's the Great Physician there.

Launch out into the deep—Luke 5:4.

One of the special marks of the Holy Spirit in the apostolic church was the spirit of boldness. One of the very essential qualities of the faith that is to attempt great things for God and expect great things from God is holy audacity. When we are dealing with a supernatural Being and taking from Him things that are humanly impossible, it is easier to take much than little; it is easier to stand in a place of audacious trust than in a place of cautious, timid clinging to the shore. Like wise seamen, let us *launch out into the deep* and find that *all things are possible to him that believeth* (Mark 9:23).

Today, let us attempt great things for God; let us take His faith to believe for them and His strength to accomplish them.

> The mercy of God is an
>   ocean divine,
> A boundless and fathomless flood;
> Launch out in the deep, cut away
>   the shoreline,
> And be lost in the fullness of God.
>
> Oh, let us launch out in this ocean
>   so broad,
> Where the floods of salvation
>   e'er flow;
> Oh, let us be lost in the mercy
>   of God,
> Till the depths of His fullness
>   we know.

According to the measure of the rule
which God hath distributed
—2 Corinthians 10:13.

A ccording *to your faith be it unto you* (Matthew 9:29), was Christ's great law of healing and blessing in His earthly ministry. This was what He meant when He said, *With what measure ye mete, it shall be measured to you again* (Matthew 7:2). These mighty measures are limited by the measures that we bring. God deals out His heavenly treasures to us in these glorious vessels, but each of us must bring our drinking cup and according to its measure we shall be filled.

But even the measure of our faith may be a divine one. Thank God, the little cup has become enlarged through the grace of Jesus until from its bottom there flows a pipe into the great ocean. And if that connection is kept open we shall find that our cup is as large as the ocean and never can be drained to the bottom. Jesus has said to us, literally, "Have the faith of God," and surely this is a limitless measure.

> Let us claim the mighty promise,
> Let us light the torches dim;
> Let us join the glorious chorus,
> Nothing is too hard for Him.

I pray not for the world, but for them—John 17:9.

How often we say we would like to have some strong Christian pray for us. In doing so we feel relieved to think that person is carrying us in his or her faith.

But there is One whose prayers never fail to be fulfilled and who is more willing to pray for us than is any human friend. His one business at God's right hand is to make intercession for His people. When we lay our burdens upon Him and claim His advocacy without doubt or fear, we are simply acknowledging the truth of His own appointment and His own definite promise and provision.

Seeing then that we have a great high priest, that is passed into the heavens, Jesus the Son of God, let us . . . come boldly unto the throne of grace, that we may obtain mercy, and find grace to help in time of need (Hebrews 4:14, 16).

> O'er the heavenly altar bending,
> Jesus interceding stands,
> All our prayers to heaven ascending,
> Reach the Father through His hands.

To abide in the flesh is more needful
for you. And having this confidence,
I know that I shall abide
—Philippians 1:24, 25.

One of the most blessed things about divine healing is that the strength it brings is holy strength. It finds its natural and congenial outflow in holy acts and exercises.

Mere natural strength seeks its gratification in natural pleasures and activities, but the strength of Christ leads us to do as Christ would do and to seek involvement in His holy service. The life of Christ in a human body saves it from a thousand temptations to self-indulgence and sin. It not only gives us strength for higher service but also a desire for it, and puts into that service a zest and spring which give it double power.

Lord, help us today to claim Thy life, and then give it for help of others.

> Have you found the branch of healing?
> Pass it on.
> Have you felt the Spirit's sealing?
> Pass it on.
> 'Twas for this His mercy sought you,
> And to all His fullness brought you,
> By the precious blood that bought you,
> Pass it on.

*He that abideth in me, and I in him, the
same bringeth forth much fruit; for
without me ye can do nothing
—John 15:5.*

So familiar are the vine and the branches, it
is not necessary to explain that the branches
and the vine are one. The vine does not say, "I am
the central trunk and you are the little
branches." Rather it acknowledges, "I am the
whole thing, and you are the whole thing."

Jesus counts us partakers of His nature. *Without me ye can do nothing.* The husband and the wife
and many other illustrations contribute to our
understanding of this marvelous teaching. It has
no parallel, no precedent in any other teaching:
that Christ is the life of His people, and we are
absolutely linked with and dependent upon Him.
All other systems teach how much man is and
may become. Christianity shows how a man
must lose all he is if he would come into full
unity with Christ in His life.

Lord, help me this day to abide in Thee.

> Oh! what a wonderful place
> Jesus has given to me!
> Saved by His glorious grace,
> I may be even as He.

Instead of the thorn shall come up
the fir tree—Isaiah 55:13.

Difficulties and obstacles are God's challenges to faith. When hindrances con-
front us in the path of duty we are to recognize
them as vessels that faith can fill with the fullness and all-sufficiency of Jesus. As we go forward, simply and fully trusting Him, we may be
tested, and we may have to wait and let
patience have her perfect work. But at last
we shall surely find the stone rolled away and
the Lord waiting to render unto us double for
our time of testing and to fulfill the promise,
Instead of the thorn shall come up the fir tree,
. . . and it shall be to the Lord for a name, for an ever-
lasting sign that shall not be cut off.

> Oft there comes a wondrous message
> When my hopes are growing dim;
> I can hear it through the darkness,
> Like some sweet and far-off hymn:
> Nothing is too hard for Jesus,
> No man can work like Him.

When my heart is overwhelmed: lead me
to the rock that is higher than I
—Psalm 61:2.

All difficulties and dangers must give way before the omnipotence of faith. By faith the walls of Jericho fell after they had been encompassed seven days, and still the mightiest citadels of the adversary must give way before the steadfast and victorious march of faith.

By faith Daniel shut the mouths of lions and was delivered, we are expressly told, because he believed in his God. It was not his uprightness of life or courageous fidelity that saved him, but his confidence in Jehovah. Such faith has held back the stroke of death and threatened disaster from many of God's children in the daily experiences of their providential lives. There is no difficulty too small for its exercise, and there is no crisis too terrible for its triumph.

Shall we go forth with this shield and buckler and prove all the possibilities of faith? Then indeed shall we possess a charmed life even through the very hosts of hell and know that we are immortal until our work is done.

I will restore to you the years that the locust hath eaten, the cankerworm, and the caterpillar, and the palmerworm, my great army which I sent among you —Joel 2:25.

A friend once said to me, "I must reap what I sowed, for God has said: *Whatsoever a man soweth, that shall he also reap.*"

"Then why don't you apply this in the spiritual world," I argued, "and compel the sinner to pay the penalty of his sins?"

Christ has borne this penalty, and the same Christ has borne the natural penalties, too, and delivered us out of condemnation in every sense. Physical sufferings come to us, not under the law of retribution but only as a divine disciple. Every penalty has been fulfilled by Christ and every law satisfied, and to the extent that we have risen with Him into the plane of spiritual and eternal life, we are lifted above the mere realm of law. We enter into the full effects of Jesus' complete satisfaction of every claim against us. So it is true that even the ruin that sin has brought upon our physical and temporal life is removed by His great atonement, and the promise is made real to us, *I will restore to you the years that the locust hath eaten.*

Be careful for nothing—Philippians 4:6.

What is the way to lay your burden down? *Take my yoke upon you, and learn of me; for I am meek and lowly in heart: and ye shall find rest unto your souls. For my yoke is easy and my burden is light* (Matthew 11:29-30). That is the way to take His burden.

We will find that Jesus' burden is always light. Our burdens are very heavy ones. It is a blessed relief if we have exchanged our burdens and laid down our loads at His blessed feet to take up His instead. God wants to rest His workers, and He is too kind to put His burden on hearts that are already bowed down with their own weight of cares.

> Are you fearing, fretting or repining?
> You can never know God's perfect
>   peace.
> On His bosom all your weight reclining,
> All your anxious doubts and cares
>   must cease.
> Would you know the peace that God
>   has given?
> Would you find the very joy of heaven?
> Be careful for nothing,
> Be prayerful for everything,
> Be thankful for anything,
> And the peace of God that passeth
>   understanding
> Shall keep your mind and heart.

The faith of the Son of God
—Galatians 2:20.

Faith is hindered most of all by what we call "our faith"—fruitless struggles to work out a faith which is but make-believe—a desperate trying to trust God that inevitably comes short of His vast and glorious promises.

The only faith that is equal to the stupendous promises of God and the measureless needs of our lives is *the faith of the Son of God* Himself. This is the very trust that Jesus will breathe into the person who intelligently accepts Him as his or her power to believe as well as to love, obey or perform any other exercise of the new life.

Blessed be the name of Jesus! He has bound us to Himself with a cord that fully reaches our poor helpless hearts, a cord that is as divine as that which binds the divine promise in the heavens. *Have the faith of God* (marginal ref. Mark 11:22) is His great command. *I live by the faith of the Son of God* is the victorious testimony of one who had proved it true.

Lord, teach me to have the faith of the Son of God.

God . . . giveth grace unto the humble
—James 4:6.

One of the marks of highest worth is deep lowliness. The shallow nature, conscious of its weakness and insufficiency, is always trying to advertise itself and make sure of its being appreciated. The strong nature, conscious of its strength, is willing to wait and let its work be made manifest in due time. Indeed, the truest natures are so free from all self-consciousness and self-consideration that their object is not to be appreciated, understood or recompensed but to accomplish their true mission and fulfill the real work of life.

One of the most suggestive expressions used respecting the Lord Jesus is given by the evangelist John in chapter 13 of his Gospel where we read, *Jesus, knowing . . . that he was come from God, and went to God; He riseth from supper . . . and began to wash the disciples' feet* (vv. 3-5). It was because He knew His high dignity and His high destiny that He could stoop to the lowest place. That place could not degrade Him.

God, give to us the divine insignia of heavenly rank: a bowed head and a meek and lowly spirit.

That I should be the minister of Jesus Christ to the Gentiles, ministering the gospel of God—Romans 15:16.

In this verse is a very beautiful and practical conception of missionary work. There is a great difference between being consecrated to our work and being consecrated to our God. We may be consecrated and fitted to do missionary work and utterly fail, if God should be calling us to do something different. When we are consecrated to God, we shall be ready for anything He may require of us. We shall be as well qualified to serve Him by the sickbed of a brother, or even in the secular duties of home, as in standing in the pulpit or leading a person to Christ.

Paul conceived his call as holy work, a special sacrifice made directly unto Christ and Christ alone. He stood as one should stand at the altar of incense, lifting up with holy hands the Gentile nations unto God. He laid all his work like fragrant incense before the throne, pleased only with what would please his Master. He dared let his work stand Jesus' inspection knowing it would have the seal of His approval in the day of judgment.

This is the spirit of true service.

Give us day by day our daily bread
—Luke 11:3.

It is impossible to live a lifetime all at once, or even in a year, but it is delightfully easy to live it a day at a time. Day by day the manna fell; so day by day we may live upon the heavenly bread and live out our lives for God. Let us, breath by breath, moment by moment, step by step, abide in Him. As we take care of the days, He will take care of the years.

God has given us two precious promises for the days. *As thy days, so shall thy strength be* (Deuteronomy 33:25) is His ancient covenant, and the literal translation of our Master's parting words to His disciples is *Lo, I am with you all the days, even unto the end of the age* (Matthew 28:20).

Observe the little water spider. Enclosed in a bubble of air it goes down beneath the surface of the pool and there builds its nest, rears its young and lives its little life in that bright sphere beneath the slimy pool. So let us in this dark world shut ourselves in with Christ in the small circle of each returning day and abide in Him, breathing the air of heaven and living in His love.

*My tongue also shall talk of thy righteous-
ness all the day long—Psalm 71:24.*

It is a simple law of nature that air always
comes in to fill a vacuum. We can produce a
draft at any time by heating the air until it
ascends, then the cold air rushes in to take its
place. Even so we can always be filled with the
Holy Spirit by providing a vacuum. This breath
is dependent upon exhausting the previous
breath before we inhale a fresh one. We must
empty our hearts of the last breath of the Holy
Spirit that we have received, for it becomes exhausted the moment we have received it, and we
need a new supply to prevent spiritual asphyxia.

We must learn the secret of breathing out as
well as of breathing in. If the first part is done
correctly, the breathing in will continue. One of
the best ways to make room for the Holy Spirit is
to recognize the needs that come into the life as
vacuums for Him to fill. We shall find plenty of
needs all around us to be filled, and as we pour
out our lives in holy service, He will pour His
in—in full measure.

Jesus, empty me and fill me
With Thy fullness to the brim.

*Out of the spoils won in battles did
they dedicate to maintain the house of
the Lord*—1 Chronicles 26:27.

Physical force is stored in the inner parts of the earth, in the coal mines and the oil deposits. So spiritual force is stored in the depths of our being, through the very pressures we cannot understand. Some day we will find that the deliverances we have won from these trials were preparing us to become true "Great Hearts" in life's *Pilgrim's Progress,* enabling us to lead our fellow pilgrims triumphantly through trial to the City of the King.

But let us never forget that the means of helping other people must be through victorious suffering. Whining and murmuring never do anybody any good. Paul did not carry a cemetery with him but a chorus choir of victorious praise. The harder the trial, the more he trusted and rejoiced, shouting from the very altar of sacrifice, *Yea, and if I be offered upon the sacrifice and service of your faith, I joy, and rejoice with you all* (Philippians 2:17).

Lord, help me this day to draw strength from all that comes to me.

Behold, I will bring evil upon all flesh,
saith the Lord: but thy life will I give
unto thee for a prey in all places whither
thou goest—Jeremiah 45:5.

The Lord's promise to Jeremiah was given for hard places. A promise of safety and life in the midst of tremendous pressure—a life for a prey.

We may well apply it to our own times, which are growing harder as we near the end of the age and the coming tribulation.

What is the meaning of *a life for a prey*? It means a life snatched from the jaws of the destroyer, as David snatched the lamb from the lion. It does not mean a place of security or of removal from the noise of battle and the presence of our foes. Rather, it means a table in the midst of our enemies, a shelter from the storm, a fortress amid the foe. It is a life preserved in the face of continual pressure. It is Paul's healing when pressed out of measure so that he despaired even of life. It is Paul's divine help when, though the thorn remained, the power of Christ rested upon him and the grace of Christ was sufficient.

Lord give me my life for a prey, and in the hardest places help me today to be victorious.

I bring you glad tidings—Luke 2:10.

A Christmas spirit should be a spirit of humility. Beside that beautiful object lesson of the manger, the cradle and the lowly little baby, what Christian heart can ever wish to be proud?

It is a spirit of joy. It is right that these should be *glad* tidings for the angel announced, *Behold, I bring you good tidings of great joy, which shall be to all people.*

It is a spirit of love. It should be the joy that comes from giving joy to others. The central fact of Christmas is the Christ who loved us and came to live among us and die for us. He or she has no right to share its joys who is living for himself or herself alone.

Love is always sacrificial, and so the Christmas spirit will call us to a glad and full surrender, first to God and then to the joyful sacrifice of what we call our own for His glory and the good of others.

The Christmas spirit is a spirit of worship. It finds the Magi at His feet with their gold and frankincense and myrrh. Let it find us there, too.

The Christmas spirit is the spirit of missions. Its glad tidings are for all people.

The spirit that dwelleth in us lusteth
to envy—James 4:5.

Though this beautiful verse has been unhappily translated in our King James version: *The spirit that dwelleth in us lusteth to envy,* it ought to be, *The spirit that dwelleth in us loveth us to jealousy.* It is a figure of a love that suffers because of its intense regard for the object loved.

The Holy Spirit is so anxious to accomplish in us and for us the highest will of God and to receive from us the truest love for Christ, our Divine Husband, that He becomes jealous when in any way we disappoint Him or give Him only our partial devotion. Therefore, God says in the preceding passage: *Ye adulterers and adulteresses, know ye not that the friendship of the world is enmity with God?*

Shall we grieve so kind a Friend? Shall we disappoint so loving a Husband? Shall we not meet the blessed Holy Spirit with the love He brings us and give in return our undivided and unbounded affection?

Was there ever a Bridegroom who loved so deeply and sought so earnestly to gain our hearts?

> *He . . . sent forth the dove; which*
> *returned not again unto him*
> *—Genesis 8:12.*

First, we see the dove going forth from the ark and finding no rest upon the wild and drifting waste of sin and judgment. This can represent the Old Testament period, when the Holy Spirit visited this sinful world but, finding no resting place, went back to the bosom of God.

Next, we see the dove going forth and returning with the olive leaf in her mouth, the symbol and the pledge of peace and reconciliation, the sign that judgment was passed and peace was returning. Surely this may beautifully represent the next stage of the Holy Spirit's manifestation, as in the ministry and death of Jesus Christ, he proclaimed reconciliation to a sinful world.

There is a third stage, when, at length the dove went forth from the ark and returned no more but made the world its home and built its nest among the habitations of men. This is the third and present stage of the Holy Spirit's work. Let us invite the Dove to make His home in our hearts.

*The Holy Ghost, whom God hath given
to them that obey him—Acts 5:32.*

We can only know and prove the fullness of the Spirit as we step out into the larger purposes and plans of Christ for the world.

Perhaps the chief reason why the Holy Spirit has been so limited in His work in the hearts of Christians is the shameful neglect of the unsaved and unevangelized world by the great majority of the professed followers of Christ. There are millions of professing Christians—and, perhaps, real Christians—in the world who have never given one real, earnest thought to the evangelization of the heathen world.

God will not give the Holy Spirit in His fullness for the selfish enjoyment of any Christian. His power is a great trust that we must use for the benefit of others and for the evangelization of the lost and sinful world. Not until the people of God begin to understand His real purpose for the salvation of men will the Church ever know the fullness of her Pentecost. God's promised power must lie along the line of duty. As we obey the command we shall receive His promise in His fullness.

Lord, help me to understand Thy plan.

*I have not shunned to declare unto you
all the counsel of God—Acts 20:27.*

It is probable that God lets every human being who crosses our path do so in order that we may have the opportunity of leaving some blessing and dropping into his heart and life some influence that will draw him nearer to God. It would be good, indeed, if ultimately we could say concerning every person whom we have ever touched in the path of life, *I am pure from the blood of all men* (Acts 20:26).

Is it really so? What about the person who sat beside us on the train? The laborer who works for us or with us? Above all, the members of our households and families? Have we done our best to lead them to Christ?

The early Christians regarded every situation as an opportunity to witness for Christ. Even when brought before kings and governors, it never occurred to them that they were to try to get free. Rather, the Master's message to them was *It shall turn to you for a testimony* (Luke 21:13). It was simply an occasion to preach to kings and rulers whom otherwise they could not reach.

That our God would . . . fulfill all the
good pleasure of his goodness, and
the work of faith with power
—2 Thessalonians 1:11.

Our God is looking today for pattern persons. When He gets a true sample, it is
very easy to reproduce him or her in other lives
without limitation.

All the experiences of life come to us as tests,
and as we meet them our loving Father is
watching with intense and jealous love to see us
overcome. If we fail He is deeply disappointed,
and our adversary is filled with joy. We are
being watched continually by angels and principalities, and every step we take is critical and
decisive for something in our eternal future.

When Abraham went out that morning to
Mount Moriah, it was an hour of solemn proba-
tion; when he came back he was one of God's
tested men, with the stamp of His eternal
approval. God could say, *I know him, that he will*
. . . do justice and judgment that the Lord may bring
upon Abraham that which he hath spoken (Genesis
18:19).

God is looking for such men and women
today. Lord, help me to be such a one.

I pray not that thou shouldest take them out of the world, but that thou shouldest keep them from the evil —John 17:15.

God wants us here on earth for some higher purpose than mere existence. That purpose is to represent Him to the world, to be the messengers of His gospel and His will to men and women, and by our lives to exhibit to them the true life and teach them how to live it.

He is representing us in heaven, and our one business is to represent Him on earth. We are just as truly sent into this world to represent Him as if we had gone to China as the ambassador of the United States government.

Although we may be engaged in the secular affairs of life, it is simply that we may represent Christ here, carry on His business and use our means to further His cause. He came here from another realm with a special message, and when His work was done He was called to go home to His Father.

Lord, help me to represent Thee worthily.

> . . . And carry music in our heart
> Through busy street and
>   wrangling mart;
> Plying our daily task with busier feet,
> Because our souls a heavenly
>   strain repeat.